The Santa Fe Trail
A Twentieth Century Excursion

The Santa Fe Trail
A Twentieth Century Excursion

Margaret Scholz Sears

SUNSTONE PRESS

SANTA FE

Sunstone books may be purchased for educational, business, or sales promotional use.
For information please write: Special Markets Department, Sunstone Press,
P.O. Box 2321, Santa Fe, New Mexico 87504-2321.

Book and cover design › R. Ahl

Printed on acid-free paper
∞

Library of Congress Cataloging-in-Publication Data

Names: Sears, Margaret Scholz, 1929- author.
Title: The Santa Fe Trail : a twentieth century excursion / by Margaret
    Scholz Sears.
Description: Santa Fe, New Mexico : Sunstone Press, 2019. | Includes
    bibliographical references. | Summary: "The journal account of a
    personal trek along the Santa Fe National Historic Trail from Franklin,
    Missouri to Santa Fe, New Mexico"-- Provided by publisher.
Identifiers: LCCN 2019024740 | ISBN 9781632932723 (paperback)
Subjects: LCSH: Sears, Margaret Scholz, 1929---Travel--Santa Fe National
    Historic Trail. | Santa Fe National Historic Trail--Description and
    travel.
Classification: LCC F786 .S43 2019 | DDC 917.804--dc23
LC record available at https://lccn.loc.gov/2019024740

WWW.SUNSTONEPRESS.COM
SUNSTONE PRESS / POST OFFICE BOX 2321 / SANTA FE, NM 87504-2321 /USA
(505) 988-4418 / ORDERS ONLY (800) 243-5644 / FAX (505) 988-1025

MADONNA OF THE TRAIL

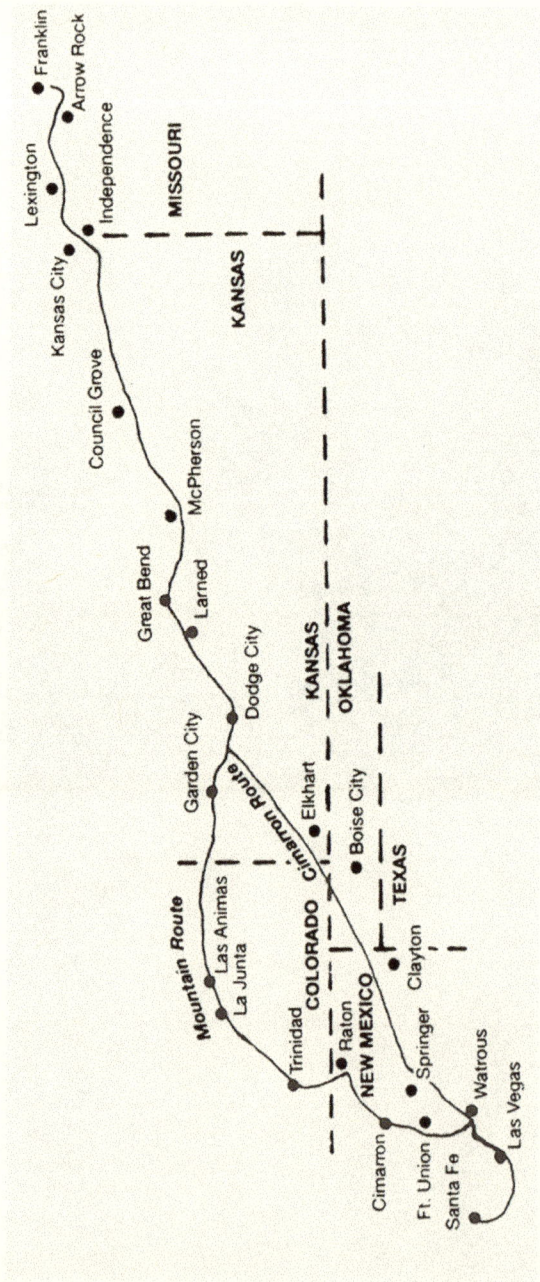

Franklin
Arrow Rock
Lexington
Independence
MISSOURI
Kansas City
KANSAS
Council Grove
McPherson
Great Bend
Larned
Dodge City
KANSAS
OKLAHOMA
Garden City
Cimarron Route
Elkhart
Boise City
TEXAS
Mountain Route
Las Animas
La Junta
COLORADO
Trinidad
Raton
NEW MEXICO
Springer
Clayton
Watrous
Cimarron
Ft. Union
Las Vegas
Santa Fe

Contents

Preface ~ 8

Introduction ~ 10

1 Scaling the Mountain Branch ~ 12

2 A High Plains Drifter in Western Kansas ~ 29

3 Trail Memories from Eastern Kansas ~ 52

4 Back to Council Grove ~ 84

5 Picking up Loose Threads ~ 97

6 Floating Across Missouri ~ 126

7 Harry's Independence ~ 157

8 Cruising Around New Mexico ~ 162

Afterword ~ 181

Bibliography ~ 182

Preface

The author of a biking book opines that pedaling the Santa Fe Trail brings one closer to the people whom one would not meet in an auto. That certainly has not been my experience over the thousands of miles I have logged in my gas chariot. If one is following the Trail, whatever the mode of transportation, one must seek out the sites and alight from one's auto, and in so doing encounter many people eager to share their small parcel of history and the experiences surrounding it. To not take the time to see the sites and talk with people would make no sense.

The advantage of travelling by auto, particularly a four wheel drive Jeep, is that few sites are too remote to explore (notwithstanding locked gates and "No Trespassing" signs). Occasionally, there is even the advantage of moving more quickly from one site to another, thereby allowing more time for communion with the Trail and its caretakers.

Such is a rather ambiguous prelude to what created my passion for the Santa Fe Trail. It began at church. I had arrived early for Sunday services, and perused a table spread with a sampling of books from the library. Purely by chance, I picked up Marc Simmons' *Following the Santa Fe Trail*.[1] Marc Simmons is undeniably the leading authority on the Santa Fe Trail and the history of the American southwest. Being new to New Mexico, and bent on learning all the state history I could absorb, this seemed a good place to commence.

Marc's "Introduction" presented in brief form the physical and abstract features that constitute the Trail. He emphasized the "force" that leads to addiction, a state that consumes "trail nuts" such a me. Reading about the Trail is no different than other educational pursuits.

I compare it with my field—music. Music literature is not music. Music is the *sound* produced by applying all that written information. By analogy, the Santa Fe Trail is not what is written on the page (or the computer). It is the feet plodding along the ruts. Marc's words drove me to put one foot before the other in a nearly two century plus year old rut in the ground. What more explanation for this journal need be made.

1. Simmons, Marc, *Following the Santa Fe Trail: A Guide for Modern Travelers*. Santa Fe, New Mexico: Ancient City Press, 1986.

Introduction

My weekend plans were set. Not to the ever-beckoning mountains to hike a tranquil trail, nor to a nearby pueblo to witness ancient Indian dances, but instead, I was going to search out the final seventy miles of the Santa Fe Trail. This was to be no dramatic pilgrimage on foot, horseback, mule, or covered wagon, but aboard my station wagon. With Marc Simmons' outstanding guidebook, *Following the Santa Fe Trail,* in hand and my dog, Demi, by my side, I headed for Las Vegas, New Mexico where excellent wagon ruts supposedly were visible. As we crested a hill north of town, there they were. I hopped from the car, ran up to the fence, and stared beyond into a sloping pasture at four parallel sets of deep scars carved into an otherwise smooth prairie. In that instant, as I was mentally transported back over a century in time, I became hooked on the Santa Fe Trail, confirming Simmons' prophesy once again. "It is a malady of mind," he said, "a compulsion, a raging addiction."[1]

With those magnificent ruts leading the way, I drove on to La Cueva, a major stop on the Mora-Las Vegas branch of the Trail. Here we strolled around an abandoned mill, whose waterwheel was motionless now, and through empty and silent red stone-walled corrals once teeming with livestock. A crumbling church, housing a to be expected resident population of pigeons in its belfry, provided the perfect picnic spot. Sitting on the steps while munching an apple, I gazed ahead at a Trail-era hacienda surrounded by quiet meadows with the majestic Sangre de Cristo mountains behind.

The hacienda and mill were built by Vicente Romero, whose high-tech irrigation system caught the attention of agriculturalists from as far away as Europe. His wagons helped create the ruts I had passed a few miles back as they transported freshly ground flour to Fort Union, fifteen miles to the east. Back to La Vegas and more ruts. No fences here, so we could place our feet where thousands of wagons and livestock had gone before. We walked around the Old Town Plaza, which now bears few reminders of Trail days. Those structures that over the years did not succumb to fire have been razed. Yet, simply knowing that from 1835 when Las Vegas was founded until the first railroad locomotive chugged into town in 1879, the ground on which we were standing was regularly a hubbub of oxen, mules, wagons, and men—a veritable Trail version of Times Square.

On to more villages, some which even today are beyond paved roads, each bearing its own unique contribution to the Trail.

Finally, home to Santa Fe and the last stop—the Plaza—where the Trail ended. Funny, as I slowly circled this present day hub of Santa Fe Activity, I did not see the skateboarders, tourists, or trim adobe shops that surrounded me, but rather, the shadowy outline of a covered wagon being drawn by lumbering oxen.

And thus began a love affair with the Santa Fe Trail which continues to this day. This essay also marked my initial literary excursion into the Trail, and the first time I was monetarily rewarded for any writing.

1. Simmons, Marc, and Joan Myers, *Along the Santa Fe Trail.* Albuquerque: University of New Mexico Press, 1986, p. xx.

1

Scaling the Mountain Branch

No sooner had I returned from my first Santa Fe Trail excursion, I was planning the next. This would be a more extended journey—to cover as much of the Mountain Route (Branch) as could be packed into four days. Because I would be traveling west to east, my first task was to determine how best to read Marc Simmons from back to front, since *Following the Santa Fe Trail* is organized from east to west. As I would discover once I hit the Trail, my organization left much to be desired. Nonetheless, I piled Demi into the car and we took off for Cimarron, New Mexico where we would pick up the Trail.

Cimarron's colorful and often violent past could easily encompass an entire volume, and, indeed, has done just that in both fiction and non-fiction. However, for my purpose, I would concentrate on the Trail first and see what drama would emanate from that.

My first stop on this pleasant May morning in 1990 was the famous St. James hotel, originally the Don Diego, built in 1875. It was witness to much violence, as confirmed by numerous bullet holes still visible in the pressed tin ceiling of the saloon. The desk clerk invited me to view several guestrooms, all which were decorated in period style. She could provide no unique accounts of Trail-related events to which the hotel was witness. However, it was apparent that such an elegant structure located in an otherwise uninhabited prairie would have surprised those who traveled this road for the first time.

I quickly moved on to the Dahl Brothers trading post and warehouse whose history tied in more closely to the period when the Mountain Route was heavily traveled. A woman drove up to the front door, eyeing me as I strolled across the abandoned original Cimarron Plaza south of the structure. I approached her, introduced myself, and explained my mission. Her name was Charlotte Fitzner, and she owned the Dahl building, which was now her home. She gave me a thumbnail history of the structure, including the most recent renovation, which Trail authorities claim has destroyed its integrity. While I was in no position to judge, I found the interior to be tastefully suited for a private residence. Yet, the red brick exterior appeared out of place both in present and past Cimarron.

Demi and I continued our walking tour of the village, pausing at the numerous buildings that created Cimarron's frenetic past. As we approached the Old Aztec Mill, built by famous Lucien B. Maxwell in 1864 and now a museum, a figure from within hung a "closed" sign on the door. Seeing me approach, he opened the door to inform me he would reopen in about two hours. Because I expected to be well down the road by then, visiting the museum would have to wait for another time.

Back in the car, we headed for Rayado. We passed the expansive Philmont Boy Scout Ranch and the elegant mansion, Villa Philmonte, formerly owned by oil magnate Waite Phillips. How desperately I wanted to get inside that mansion, but the summer tourist season, when the house was open, was still a few weeks distant. I stopped at the Ranch museum, hoping to learn more about the Trail in the vicinity. The director, Steve Zimmer, introduced himself and invited me into his office, eager to talk about the Trail. He unrolled a huge topographical map, and with his finger charted the Trail, or rather trails, because at least two branches descend into Rayado from U.S. 64 east of Cimarron. In addition to the visible ruts Simmons notes, he pointed out a fine trace south of Rayado which I definitely should not miss. Not having forgotten the mansion I had just passed, I asked if I could tour the grounds. Not only did he reply in the affirmative, but since it was being readied to open, the house manager might allow me inside.

For the moment though, my course was set south to see ruts and Rayado, a mere ghost town save for Kit Carson's house built in 1849 and now also a museum—closed—and the first house Lucien Maxwell built in this locale. Considering the vast number of houses Carson is claimed to have occupied or visited, he may have rivaled George

Washington in the number of beds reputedly slept in.

Farther south the highway makes a broad ninety degree left turn, and it was just beyond this turn that I spied that broad swale on the right side heading southwest for Fort Union. Indeed, Steve was right by insisting that I see these beautiful ruts. Unfortunately, I had to be content to view them from the road because they were behind a barbed wire fence. I gazed first with binoculars then the naked eye, back and forth until other ruts farther up the Mountain Route beckoned me. And, of course, there was Villa Philmonte.

At the mansion I discovered many busy workers. Yes, I was permitted to go inside. I softly walked up the broad staircase into a grand living room, (or was it a ballroom?). The decoratively painted ceiling beams and intricately carved corbels particularly caught my attention in this elegant room filled with exotic antiques. I moved slowly from room to magnificent room. The manager was nowhere to be found. I worked my way to the dining wing where I heard a voice. Following the sound I came upon the office where a woman was talking on the telephone. When I explained my purpose, she graciously led me through the remainder of the mansion, giving a most polished description of the history of house and contents. As I walked over to the nine foot grand piano for a closer look, she stated that it was a player piano, which astounded me, and rightly so because only five were ever built.

After roaming about for ever so long, I profusely thanked my guide and exited to the spacious grounds which boasted acres upon acres of electric green grass. After spending much of the day sleeping in the car, Demi was ready for a romp on that cool lawn. I made a note of yet another spectacular spot to visit when it was officially open. Yet, not even a presumably more detailed interpretation (the manager's words) by a tour guide could begin to compare with my private viewing of this transplanted Mediterranean villa.

Back on U.S. 64 heading for Raton, ruts were sighted from time to time paralleling the road. I stopped at the National Rifle Association building to inquire the whereabouts of a Daughters of the American Revolution (DAR) marker on the grounds. Finally, the third person I queried knew about it. It could best be approached from the highway upon climbing a fence. Either the directions were incorrect or I misunderstood them. Whatever, I never located the marker. The Clifton House hotel ruins was the next site I missed, choosing not to tramp through the rattlesnake infested overgrowth the three-quarters mile to its location beyond the Canadian River.

Raton was my first night's stop, so I immediately located a motel, then set out for Willow Springs, the site of a stage station and ranch. The spring is now in the back yard of a tidy white frame bungalow. I walked to the fence surrounding the property and peered across a well manicured, luxuriant lawn and garden. Mary Gaskin, the owner, came from the house and invited me into the backyard to see the spring, which is now capped. The abundantly flowing spring currently provides water for the expansive lawn and garden. How blessed to have a constant supply of good water under one's feet here in the arid southwest. However, the reality for Mary and husband Willie is that the grounds require much too much work for retirement aged persons such as themselves.

We chatted about the Trail, and Mary pointed to a small cabin in the backyard that was the original stage station. She showed me a photo of the structure taken when the station was actively servicing travelers heading up to or down from Raton Pass along the Trail.

Eventually our conversation shifted to local families. My husband was born in Raton, and although his family moved away when he was four years old, relatives still reside here. Yes, she knew the family and was able to pinpoint where each presently as well as formerly resided. Such is the richness of small-town living. Thus ended my first day on the Mountain Route.

Trinidad, Colorado was my first destination on day two. A scenic overlook atop Raton Pass, halfway between these two towns, allowed me my first view of the snow-capped Spanish Peaks, the imposing twin landmarks which guided westbound wagon trains for many days. I was viewing them from the other direction, but they easily could guide travelers heading for other destinations.

Trinidad is nestled among hills, and I could well imagine the difficulties that posed during winter snows. I stopped at the historic Baca and Bloom houses, finding both closed, so I drove to the Colorado

Visitors Center for assistance. Neither residence would be open until the beginning of June, I was informed, but students were working at the former that morning, and I might be granted access. The Visitors Center host made several telephone calls and learned that I would probably find someone there in a few hours. Then I asked if perchance I might be able to visit "Uncle Dick" Wootton's ranch. Wootton was the irascible entrepreneur and engineer who built a toll road over Raton Pass in 1866 which greatly eased the treacherous journey that plagued early travelers.

The road that existed prior to "Uncle Dick's" engineering wonder was no road at all, but merely a crude mule trail which wound up, over, and around boulders and crevasses. Susan Magoffin vividly described the exhausting struggle. A day's journey, she wrote, was measured in yards, not miles.

The Visitors Center host again dialed the telephone, checking if I might be allowed on the Wootton ranch property. No one answered, but he was willing to try again when I would be back this way in a few days.

When I returned to the Baca house at the appointed time there was no sign of workers about, so I had to abandon any hope of touring this fine house. It was time to "noon," and what better spot than the Kit Carson Park high atop a hill overlooking the city. At the center of the park sits a fine equestrian statue of Kit, looking down on all of Trinidad from astride his prancing steed.

My next objective was Marion Russell's home and grave in Stonewall (or Picketwire as it is also known), about forty miles west of Trinidad. Marion, whose classic memoirs are recorded in her book, *Land of Enchantment,* made her first of five journeys across the Trail at the tender age of seven years. This detour from the Trail was mandatory, for to speak her name is to automatically think, "Santa Fe Trail." Entering the village was synonymous with exiting it, for only a general store with fishing resort behind marked the spot where Marion raised her family. I wound my way up the dirt road to the cemetery which sits in a grove of ponderosa pine on the brow of a hill. I strolled among the tombstones in this well maintained, fenced final resting place for the pioneers who settled this, the St. John's valley.

I gazed at the headstone marking Marion's grave and, like so many others before me, was moved by the inspired setting. "Thank you, Marion," I said, "for sharing your life with us."

My gaze shifted to the view of the apple green meadow below from whence the muted lowing of cattle floated up the hill. I will let Marion continue describing the scene spread before me as she first saw it. "Mid-afternoon...we saw the great Stone Wall rising from the blue mists at its feet. Behind it, with all its towers and turrets, rose the white-capped Sangre de Cristo Mountains ... meaning Blood of Christ .... [W]e thought [they] were well named, for their snowy tops were stained blood-red by the setting sun."[1]

Returning from some mesmerizing shadowland into which I had been drawn, I looked about for Demi. She was standing at the cemetery gate, and no amount of coaxing could force her to walk into this resting place of the dead. Back at the gate I looked about on the ground for a rock to take home as a keepsake. A common igneous moss rock seemed perfect, so I picked up one of the many strewn about.

Reluctantly, I pulled myself away from this special place. (How often on future Trail journeys would I echo these same words.) Time was fleeing, and there were many stops to make before reaching La Junta, Colorado, my "campground" for the night.

Reading Simmons' guide in reverse order caused me to unknowingly miss several sites. However, I did not miss Hole-in-the-Rock, a deep hole filled with a constant supply of water. At least that was so until the Atchison, Topeka, and Santa Fe Railroad filled it in when nearby Timpas Creek was dammed to create a source of water for its mighty steam engines. I was greeted by a pack of noisy dogs as I pulled into the drive of a modest ranch house which fronted the ruins of the Hole-in-the-Rock Overland Stage Station. A youngish bearded man came from the house in response to the racket. Yes, he had heard that a ruined barn behind the house might possibly be said station. Although I wanted to tramp around the barn, the presence of livestock in the adjoining corral and some inner premonition stilled my voice. I thanked him and drove away. Perhaps when I am next in the vicinity the vibes will be more positive and I will not hesitate to ask permission for a closer look.

Note: Indeed, such occurred in 2007 on a Santa Fe Trail Association (SFTA) symposium Trail tour. We walked to the stage station ruins and throughout the meadows and boulders that bordered several catchment pools for the headwaters of Timpas Creek.

Trail travelers over the years expressed varying opinions of the Creek waters and surroundings, a slightly wooded spot amidst hot, bare, and dry southeastern Colorado. The general impression of Kearny's Army of the West heading for battle in New Mexico as the Mexican-American war commenced, was a disappointment. Word had spread along the Trail of a "crystal font" wending its way through a "beautiful and fragrant meadow" when, in fact, there were but a few holes containing a little filthy water.[2] James Ross Larkin, a frail young man from St. Louis seeking health in Santa Fe, found the water at the Hole good. Certainly, one who was aware of any anomalies to his physiological system would recognize bad water.[3] These property owners on the day we visited were new since my first experience. They warmly welcomed us and joined us on the tour of the site. What a pleasant contrast. Now to return to that earlier excursion.

There were no negative vibes when I pulled into the ranch drive below Iron Spring Stage Station. I was greeted by two pre-school mounted cowboys. Immediately I was impressed with these youngsters' equestrian skills. Their mother came from the house and graciously allowed me to walk to the spring which was located beside the road I had just passed. She also suggested I walk into the field opposite to a Daughters of the American Revolution marker which signaled well-defined ruts. The station is now marked only by a few foundation stones and fence post stubs from the nearby long since disappeared corral. As I gazed about the expanding prairie, the Spanish Peaks which had been over my left shoulder most of the day were in full view, clear of the haze that usually surrounds them. It was appropiate that such a sight should bring to an end a very full day.

The next morning we left La Junta early enough to be at the Bent's Old Fort gate when it opened. Bent's Fort, that most famous of all western trading posts, was the creation of brothers Charles and William Bent and Ceran St. Vrain. From 1833 until 1848 they not only controlled much of the economic activity in the southwest from within its walls but, most importantly, influenced and shaped relations among Indians, Hispanics, and Anglos. As I toured this famous edifice, which is actually a reproduction of the original, built by the National Park Service (NPS), my mind was a whirl of descriptions written by those who had been inside its original walls—Susan Magoffin, Louis Garrard, Matt Field among the most notable.

From the bastion platform one could look out over the vast prairie which was level on the east but rose to a gentle bluff on the north. To the south flowed the Arkansas River, once again heavily wooded with cottonwood trees after having been stripped clean during the Trail days. Scanning the horizon 360 degrees, I found myself in the middle of a déjà vu experence, the feeling that one has experienced a given situation previously. But, this was my first visit to the Fort. However, I had read many accounts by Trail travelers/authors as well as David Lavender's outstanding history of the Fort. These writers had impressed a definitive picture of the area in my brain, a picture which was familiar when my eyes took in the actual scene for the first time. At the risk of sounding metaphysical, I tend to believe that something besides highly graphic literary talents was in operation. Leaving the Fort, I passed a reedy marshland which was alive with the cacophonous chattering of clouds of birds—redwing blackbirds, which I recognized, and many other species which I did not. I made a note to pack bird and flower books with the Trail guides in the future.

The remainder of the day was spent in Las Animas and Boggsville. My batting average continued to register zero in attempting to find "open" museums—Kit Carson museum was closed. Boggsville now hardly qualifies even as a ghost own, and even though I was carefully following Simmons' map, the turn off easily could be missed. The heavily deteriorated remnants of only two houses still stand. But, these are significant to Trail history, for they were owned by Santa Fe Trail traders—one by John Prowers and the other, Thomas Boggs. I encountered members of the local historical society being guided through the Boggs house. One of their number told me that, unfortunately, I could not enter the unstable structure. However, restoration would soon be underway, and if I returned in a few years I would be rewarded. With my luck, even when the job is completed, I will probably visit on a day it is *not* open.

After paying my respects at William Bent's grave in the Boggsville cemetery, I turned west and headed back toward Santa Fe. The noble Spanish Peaks were now before me rather than over my shoulder mile after mile. It was hard to believe that from first sight, when almost hidden in haze, until they disappeared behind Raton Pass, less than two hours of driving was required. For Trailers, however, the landmarks would be visible for four to five days. J.T. Fraser, the eminent authority on the interdisciplinary study of time, believes we are living in a "time-compact" world in which our experience of time is compressed due to the influence of high technology. Perhaps the dichotomy of the Spanish Peaks as experienced while walking beside an oxen-drawn wagon as against from behind the wheel of an automatic drive Buick station wagon is an apt analogy of Fraser's premise.

The 85 miles between La Junta and Trinidad is a rather desolate stretch of highway. Not even my beloved pronghorn antelope could be found. Thus, the Spanish Peaks provided an aesthetic image upon which to focus, and the promise of many mountains ahead quickened my heart, as it must have the Trail travelers.

A few miles north of Trinidad I turned off the highway toward Hoehne. A sign reading "Home of the Santa Fe Trail Ruts" held promise of more ruts. I turned to Franzwa's guide only to discover that after the third turn I was hopelessly lost in a maze of unusually numbered roads, not all congruent with his numbering. Now, Hoehne's population is but two hundred people. How could one become lost in such a tiny hamlet? Very easily, I discovered. A pedestrian approached, so I inquired where the Trail was. He shook his head and said he was new in town. I drove on a short distance and encountered several children. They were no help either. Finally, I spotted an elderly gentleman emerging from a small corral. Now I would be successful. He thought he knew where the ruts were, but upon following his directions I found I had come full circle and still no sign of ruts. I could not even locate a viable business establishment where I could at least discover who had erected the sign at the highway. Because I still wanted to try again to go to "Uncle Dick" Wootton's ranch, I had to abandon any further attempt. Greg Franzwa, I suggest a map of Hoehne in your guidebook, small though the town is, would be far better help to us Trail trekkers than the difficult to follow written directions.

Back at the Visitors Center in Trinidad the hospitable host again tried to gain permission for me to visit Wootton's ranch, but again the telephone rang and rang—no answer. Possibly, the most valuable attributes required of those wandering around in search of the Trail are patience and time. One must possess an abundance of both, not always easy for impatient Americans. However, for persons who allow events to unfold naturally, and do not become anxious because control is not in their hands, the rewards are immeasurable.

It was noon, so again I headed up the hill to cool and green Kit Carson Park where we once again enjoyed a picnic lunch under the stern gaze of the bronze "dean" of the West. Although it was only mid-afternoon when we arrived in Raton, twenty-one miles farther down the Trail, I decided we would spend the night there, thereby allowing ample time to revisit the sites I had toured three days earlier, as well as other local attractions such as the railroad depot and the well known Schuler theatre. The latter contains a ceiling mural which includes several panels drawn from Santa Fe Trail days. This being Sunday, the building was locked. But I was able to catch a glimpse through the glass doors leading into the lobby. (As I reread this several years later, I realize I have not yet gotten inside that theatre, although I have passed through Raton a number of times. Next time.)

The next morning we headed for Fort Union, stopping at Wagon Mound en route. The mound which hovers above the village bears the same name, and was one of the major landmarks toward which caravans aimed. Can you imagine the astonishment of the first-time traveler as he stared at the silhouette of a perfectly formed covered wagon being drawn by a pair of low-slung oxen? Upon entering town I stopped to view a bronze engraved plaque depicting William Becknell's first pack train across the Trail. It is one of only two such markers, the other being at Pawnee Rock in Kansas. The town, it seems, is distinguished for more than a unique geological formation.

I drove on to Santa Clara cemetery, which sits alongside Hillside cemetery at the very base of the stone Wagon Mound. The view of the promontory is spread unfettered before the viewer and, misleadingly, appears to require but a short uphill jaunt to the summit. The gravestone I was searching for was that of Charles Fraker, a freighter. The stone contains an exquisitely carved oxen-drawn wagon. However, I will have to take Simmons' word for it because the cemetery gates were locked. Imagine.

The road leading to Fort Union upon exiting I-25 at Watrous is bounded on both sides by "awesome" ruts heading for Santa Fe. Had they not been behind fences, we certainly would have taken a walk.

By the time we had arrived at the Fort, the sun's rays were rapidly heating up, too warm for Demi to tour the ruins. I reminded her that she had been here before, therefore she could take a nap without missing a new experience. I located a shady parking space, cracked the car windows, and took a quick jaunt around the "jewel of the west." A fine swale heading toward the Visitors Center was marked. Although posted signs instructed me to stay on the path, I could not resist walking a few yards along that ancient road, admitting my transgression to a park ranger. He pointed me toward more dramatic ruts on the periphery of the complex that I was free to stroll for some distance.

In the Visitors Center I asked another ranger if he knew where Marion Russell and her U.S. Army officer husband, Richard, had lived. It was at this Fort Marion and Richard were married and where she set up the first of many households in her beloved southwest. Records had not been found, I was told, which specified the quarters inhabited by junior officers. The prospect of engaging in a search was mighty tempting.

But now it was time to move on and check out Tiptonville on the Fort Union road, a mile plus north of Watrous, which, despite its ghost-town appearance, is inhabited—by other than humans as well, I would discover. Tiptonville was founded about 1870 by William Tipton, Samuel Watrous' son-in-law. I slowly drove down one dusty road after another. At one corner I looked ahead to see a peacock proudly strutting across the road. He appeared to have come from the ruins of the Masonic Lodge, and was headed toward the few remains of Rev. Thomas Harwood's Methodist mission school, both structures which existed in the era of the Trail.

It was now midafternoon (again), and both Demi and I were becoming weary. But, there was one more stop I hoped to make—the church at San Miguel del Vado. It had not been open on my previous visits, and I hoped this time I would fare better. However, construction was underway at the exit from I-25 leading to the village. I decided that if traffic was halted I would continue on to Santa Fe. Luckily, it was not. So I drove the three miles to San Miguel and pulled into the church parking lot behind another car, which appeared to have been physically lifted from John Steinbeck's novel, *Grapes of Wrath,* depicting the devastating drought and dust bowl of the1930s that struck much of the nation's midsection. A man exited from the solidly packed auto in which a woman and two small children were also tightly squeezed. He asked if I knew where the local priest lived. When I responded in the negative, he told me his sad tale. The family was heading back home to Colorado following the loss of his job in Las Cruces. The car was almost out of gas, and he was penniless. The convenience store clerk at the I-25 exit suggested he might find work in San Miguel.

While we talked, another car pulled up and three women emerged. As they started up the steps to the campo santo, I asked if they knew where the priest lived. The stranded man then told them his story. One of the ladies was astounded anyone would suggest work was available in this tiny, sleepy village. I gave the man ten dollars and suggested he locate a homeless shelter in Las Vegas where he would find help. The ladies also pressed money into his palm, and we all wished the family well.

As I drove away I mused, if the man had *not* driven off I-25 down to sleepy San Miguel but, instead, headed back onto the interstate, would he have been as fortunate? That day I had no better success gaining entrance to the church, but the drama that unfolded from the last minute decision to chance it far outweighed the privilege of viewing the sanctuary. Such are the experiences one encounters on the Santa Fe Trail.

Notes

1. Russell, Marion Sloan. *Land of Enchantment: Memoirs of Marian Russell Along the Santa Fe Trail as Dictated to Mrs. Hal Russell.* Albuquerque, New Mexico: University of New Mexico Press, 1981, p. 129.

2. Hyslop, Stephen G. *Bound for Santa Fe: The Road to New Mexico and the American Conquest, 1806–1848.* Norman, Oklahoma: University of Oklahoma Press, 2002, p. 333.

3. Barbour, Barton H. (Ed.). *Reluctant Frontiersman: James Ross Larkin on the Santa Fe Trail 1856–1857.* Albuquerque, New Mexico: University of New Mexico Press, 1990, p. 92.

Marion Russell's grave, Picketwire, Colorado.

Bent's Fort, La Junta, Colorado.

Spanish Peaks, Southern Colorado.

Wagon Mound, New Mexico.

Charles Fraker's grave, Wagon Mound Cemetery, Wagon Mound, New Mexico.

2

A High Plains Drifter in Western Kansas

Following the Santa Fe Trail had become a passion with me, thus by the time I made plans to tour the western Kansas segment, I was a confirmed "rut nut" and my knowledge had greatly expanded. Granted, I had a long way to go to match the many Trail buffs who had been "on the Trail" many more years than I. I had not attended symposia of the SFTA, but did join the Association and its local chapter, the End of the Trail. My ability to identify ruts had improved, but I could still easily be misled. I had not yet acquired the passion to locate and photograph every Daughters of the American Revolution marker—that would come later. Of course, I did search for all that my guidebooks listed. As for a camera, I had given up photography shortly after moving to Santa Fe, and I believe I "see" more now than I did when my eye was glued against the viewfinder rather than freely roaming the horizon.

Demi and I had been visiting family in Wichita, and decided to take the Trail route home. On a crisp October morning in 1990 I bade them goodbye and headed for McPherson where I would pick up the Trail. Nothing spectacular was to be seen there. However, I did log my first Kansas DAR marker and Mormon Battalion plaque. Five miles south of McPherson I located the marker and a Kansas historical plaque commemorating the Dry Turkey Creek Treaty between the U.S. and the Kansas (Kaw) tribe. The treaty guaranteed wagon trains permission to cross Kaw lands. The creek proper was about a mile west of the markers.

Farther down the highway I turned onto a county road and aimed for the Little Arkansas River crossing. To get to the riverbank I had to hike across a plowed field. The bank was quite overgrown with underbrush, bushes, and trees. So much so that the marker identifying the actual crossing was hard to locate. As I tramped through the brush I sang and talked loudly, making a significant amount of noise to alert snakes and other unfriendly critters that I was in the neighborhood. Although I did locate the marker, not so any water.

Despite the river's modest width, only five to six yards by Josiah Gregg's reckoning, its steep banks and miry bed made crossing an arduous task. He described the engineering operation necessary here and at other crossings. "It is the practice," he wrote in *The Commerce of the Prairies*, "for several men to go in advance with axes, spades, and mattocks and by digging the banks and erecting temporary bridges to have all in readiness by the time the wagons arrive."[1] And to think, they repeated the process time and again across the entire length of the Trail.

My next stop was at a nearby farmhouse to ask permission to enter their pasture to see a fine array of Trail ruts. It was here that I met the first of a number of friendly and gracious people who not only assisted me but brought new meaning to my journey, that being, encounters with sharing and caring people who are part of the Santa Fe Trail experience. Of course, having lived in the midwest most of my life, I was no stranger to the gregariousness of its natives. This journey confirmed for me the heartwarming reassurance that Kansans have not changed.

A pair of classic farm dogs greeted me exuberantly as I drove up to the farmhouse. Soon a lady emerged from the house wearing a broad smile. When I explained my mission, she broke into a long discussion about this section of the Trail. She wanted to go with me to her ruts, but was in the midst of preparing dinner—that is the midday meal in farm country—for the menfolk who were expected momentarily from the fields. She invited me into her house, partly to show me a book about the Trail she thought I should acquire, and partly to show off her living room. The room was quite large in distinctively western style. A huge stone fireplace occupied one corner. The walls were covered cheek to jowl with animal trophies, framed arrowheads, family photos, and original artwork from the area. A brightly colored patterned area rug gathered into a large circle the massive western-style overstuffed furniture. It was a room that showed the wear of a family that was content with its life and fortune.

Reluctantly, I said my goodbye and drove to the edge of the pasture to view the ruts. They were not as distinct as I had expected, and the iron cross marker supposedly in their midst could not be located. However, trusting Simmons' description in *Following the Santa Fe Trail,* I feel confident that what I saw were bona fide ruts.

After locating several more DAR markers, I stopped at an ancient stone schoolhouse known as the Stone Corral school because its building material came from the long since dismantled Stone Corral, the site which I had passed a few miles east. The dilapidated condition of the roof, windows, and doors gave testimony to its neglect since it was closed in 1946. But, the sturdy stone walls verified that it was not yet ready to melt into the earth, providing it received help.

A few miles farther west I entered the town of Lyons and stopped at the local museum. After viewing the small Trail exhibit, I started to leave. The docent informed me that a fine exhibit covering other aspects of the area's history was on a lower floor. I explained that I could not leave my dog in the car any longer. No problem, the kind gentleman remarked, Demi was welcome to come in. In thirty years of dog ownership, I cannot recall any of my dogs being invited into a museum. Once again mid-western hospitality was warmly extended, and this time to a Bulldog.

Time for lunch, and since our next stop, the Father Padilla monument, was located in a small roadside park nearby, we "nooned" there. Father Juan de Padilla accompanied Don Francisco Vasquez de Coronado on the latter's search for the fabled Seven Cities of Cibola in 1541. It was in this section of Kansas that Coronado realized there were no cities of gold. Today, we know that, indeed, there is gold in Kansas. It is called "wheat."

We had now entered the most dangerous section of the Trail, which extended from Cow Creek to Pawnee Rock. However, today we were not on the lookout for an ambush, but for ruts on another farmer's property. I drove into a quiet farm yard which displayed no evidence of activity. Not expecting any response to my knock, I was surprised when the door opened and an elderly gentleman with gleaming silver hair cut in contemporary style midway down his neck stood on the other side. Rather than point me in the right direction, he donned a jacket and personally escorted me on a tour of his ruts. We entered a shelter belt, a twenty-five foot or so wide band of trees which plains farmers plant to protect their crops from the ever-blowing winds. Walt (Sharp)—we were now on a first name basis—explained that he had planted these trees long before he knew the Trail passed his way When he learned of the important history that had unfolded on his property, he was sorry about the trees. However, as time passed he realized that because of the foliar covering, the beautiful swales had been totally protected as much so as would have a blanket.

The tour did not end here. Walt asked if I had ever seen buffalo wallows, which I had not. "I thought not" he replied gleefully. He led me to a collection of faint oval depressions that were darker in color than the surrounding ground cover. We moved on to more wallows and ruts which ended at a freshly plowed field. All the while, he chatted about the good, yet hard life he and his family had lived on the farm. Yes, he had lived on this site all of his life except for two years spent in Kansas City when he was young. He found the big city was too rough and dangerous, and he was eager to return to the tranquility and freedom of rural living. The farm was now being worked by his sons, but he thought he might go back to work so he would have more free time. All the while, Walt was smoking, and I doubt that this spry octogenarian—or older—gave even passing attention to the cancer warnings we technologically sophisticated people worry over daily.

Another farmer, who had been plowing a nearby field, alighted from his tractor and came over to join our tour. Between the two, they told me of all the other Trail sites in the area I should visit. As hard as it was, eventually I had to pull myself away from this charming, silver-headed sprite who had granted me the privilege of sharing a tiny moment of his life.

Next stop was "Ralph's Ruts," no doubt the most famous collection of ruts on the Trail. They have been beautifully preserved in a pasture by the property owner, Ralph (Hathaway), of course. I stopped on the road beside broad swales which stretched far into the pasture. The presence of a huge Black Angus bull close to the fence convinced me I should view the ruts from what I hoped was the safety of my car. He stared unblinking at me, and I smiled back.

On the opposite side of the road a DAR marker supposedly was located. I drove up and down a section of the fence several times, but could not locate it. I still was unwilling to *walk* the fence for a closer look, not with Mr. Macho leering at me from the other side of the road. My attention returned to him. He strolled up to the fence, pawed the ground with a sturdy hoof, emitted a snort or two, and turned his head to one side. I looked more closely and realized he was pointing directly at the marker, which was at the tip of his nose. I could almost hear him grumble, "Simmons goofed. The marker is on *this* side of the road, and this lady is never going to find it without my help." My next stop was farther down this road, but at the first intersection I doubled back to get yet another look at Mr. Macho. He was still standing where I left him by the marker.

Several years later while visiting a friend, Ruth Boxberger, in Great Bend, I took her to see these dramatic ruts. By then the bull and his buddies had been replaced by a few mellow-appearing horses. A small parking area had been constructed, beside which was a gate inviting viewers into the pasture where they could walk a few hundred yards among ruts and thus into history. As we strolled about, Ralph Hathaway drove up to welcome us and show us where the best photo could be taken. He pointed out several parallel ruts. Four are common from central Kansas westward, but seven are most unusual. He explained that the soil is quite sandy here, and the ever-present winds filled the tracks with loose soil, thereby minimizing traction. To counteract this impediment, the trace was periodically moved laterally to firm soil.

We chatted about many things: ruts, both in this pasture and on his son's land due west; artifacts he had found, particularly in the vicinity of the infamous Plum Butts massacre; the Santa Fe Trail Association; and other Trail related topics. Ralph pointed toward a grove of trees about a mile east of his ruts as the site of the Plum Buttes massacre, although the buttes themselves are 1½ miles west of where we stood. Apparently, the name was attached to the grizzly event because the buttes were the closest landmark. The incident occurred in 1867 when the wagon train of a trader named Franz Huning was attacked by Cheyenne Indians. Huning's mother-in-law, her young son, and a driver were killed in the fray.

Appearing in no hurry to leave, Ralph was more than willing to share his considerable knowledge and passion for his "one-half mile of Santa Fe Trail" (I borrowed the phrase from the title of the booklet he authored). He encouraged us to drive by Gunsight Notch 1.5 miles west of his ruts. This romantic sounding sobriquet was a distinct saddle in a gentle rise that had been created over time by thousands of wagon wheels. Ruts were visible on both sides of the hill. Just north of this formation are the Plum Buttes themselves.

Ruth's excitement level was rising as we roamed those section line roads. I could well imagine her returning to these sites in the near future with family and/or friends in tow.

To return to that October day in 1990—Plum Buttes, Fort Zarah, Walnut Creek Crossing—on I drove realizing time and again that the hundred miles I had covered in less than eight hours would have required six to seven days by wagon train. Caravans averaged fifteen miles per day. That average was easily surpassed on this section except when storms slowed or even temporarily halted fording numerous streams that crossed the Trail, or when encounters with hostile Indians or bushwackers occurred. Prairie fires could also interrupt a caravan's progress, not to mention consume it in its horrific embrace.

Even before I turned into the grounds of the Barton County museum in Great Bend, I knew that it was closed for the day. That was to be my fate for the other three museums on my list of planned stops—too early, too late, or closed for the weekend. My next Trail trek will be scheduled around these rather than the other way around. There were other missed sites, such as the Allison-Peacock Trading Post which is located on private property. The only life I could raise there from my repeated knocks on the door were a Basset Hound and an unclassifiable black dog who were frantically racing around the trunk of a huge cottonwood tree. Whatever creature they had treed was not visible in its many leafy branches.

Note #1: Four years later when I again stopped here, only the dogs had changed—still no one at home. However, fortune did smile on me in another way, for the Barton County museum was open. The Trail exhibit included a fine miniature model of the Allison-Peacock Trading Post. Considering the bad luck I have experienced at the actual site, the model may be the closest I will ever come to seeing it.

Note #2: Fast forward to 2009, almost two decades from my first attempted visit to the Allison-Peacock Trading Post. Faye Gaines and I were again traveling together, this time to the Santa Fe Trail Association symposium in Arrow Rock, Missouri. We had spent the night in Great Bend, so the Trading Post and the two Fort Zarah sites, which are located at the great bend of Walnut Creek, were on our route east. Of course, I had slim expectations of finding anyone at home, thus I was amazed when a man responded to my knock. Yes, there were a few remaining foundation stones, he said, pointing in the direction of a collection of farm vehicles amid high weeds beyond a barn. We tromped through the weeds, but unfortunately, were looking in the wrong direction. Greg Brown, the owner, eventually came to our rescue and located them for us. He also pointed out the site where a few decades ago the remains of ten teamsters who were killed at the infamous Walnut Creek massacre were located. He has lived his entire life in this immediate area, and has many memories of playing in and about the first Fort Zarah, which is a few hundred yards west of the trading post. At that time, the ground south of the fort was littered with artifacts.

The Walnut Creek Massacre occurred on July 18, 1864 during which ten teamsters—eight white and two black—were killed by a band of Kiowa and Arapaho Indians. However, it was not until 1973 that remains were recovered along the creek bank. It has not been confirmed that these are the same ten men killed in 1864, but strong evidence indicates they are.[2] Greg remembered the exhumation, and probably participated.

Having found a captive audience, Greg took us first to a barn to show off his 1947 restored maroon Ford coupe and then to a kennels housing three registered German Shepherd dogs, one who had recently given birth to a litter. From the "nursery" he brought out two of the squirming babies, one tan and the other silver, for us to hold. Perhaps he thought these two mature women could not resist cuddly puppies, and that a sale might be in the offing. Some things are worth waiting for, and this visit to Allison-Peacock Trading Post is definitely one of those. Now to return to that 1990 journey.

I was now in short grass prairie, the land of the bison. Looking about at the level terrain which extended as far as the eye could see and beyond, it was difficult to comprehend that until the 1870s this land was often black with bison, also as far as the eye could see. In his diary, David Kellogg used such terms as "buffalo aplenty," "hordes of buffalo," and "buffalo very plentiful." Dr. Michael Speck appeared unable to adequately describe the scene which must have overwhelmed him when he wrote, "To say we saw thousands [of buffalo] would give an imperfect idea of their numbers and to say we saw One Hundred Thousand acres of land covered with them will give a better idea, but still would fall short of the truth."[3] He further went on to claim that bison were in sight for over four hundred miles along the Trail. Again I stared all about me, and I still cannot believe they are all gone.

Pawnee Rock was the next important stop on my route. The Pawnee tribe used the rock as a lookout during their raids against the Sioux—hence the origin of its name.[4] It was the only rock outcropping on the otherwise flat plains that extended (once again, to repeat) as far as the eye could see. Although a major landmark, it is more memorable as the site of numerous ambushes, for this was hostile Indian territory. Most Trail writers had more than passing remarks to record about this spot. Today the Rock is contained within a small park which is administered by the Kansas State Historical Society. A circle drive took me to the crest. There, are located an impressive obelisk-style monument and an observation platform. At the top of the platform I was rewarded with a stunning view of unbroken prairie. When caravans were moving along the Trail, the Rock reached a height approximating where I was standing at the top of the fifteen foot platform. However, later the railroad and homesteaders used the solid stone for construction purposes.

I climbed among the many rocks at the base of Pawnee Rock, looking for authentic carved signatures of travelers from among the mass of graffiti of more recent and less memorable vintage. I found one—I think. Regretfully, it was not Susan Magoffin's. On the morning of July 4, 1846 she had quickly pecked her name as the caravan was commencing the day's march, with husband Sam standing watch above and her maid guarding her in front. "It was not well done," she wrote later, "for fear of Indians made me tremble all over and I hurried it over in any way.[5] Also among those autographs are two handsome bronze plaques. One commemorates the Trail and the other William Becknell's inaugural trip to Santa Fe in 1821. The latter is one of only two such plaques, the other being located at Wagon Mound, New Mexico.

This site was not to be vacated too quickly because of the view and the images it conjured in the mind's eye. Many opportunities for ambush abounded. Coupled with that was the great distance against which an approaching caravan could be easily spotted. I tried to visualize such, but the twentieth century kept intruding. My fantasies were further interrupted by a police patrol car that came cruising through the park. (At least, he did not have a ghetto blaster.)

Before entering the Larned complex, my next planned stop, I took another gravel road to Ash Creek Crossing where later on that Independence Day in 1846 Susan's carriage capsized fording the creek. A fellow and his dog were on bridge as I approached. I stopped to ask if he knew about the crossing and the nearby campground. His Trail knowledge was a bit hazy, he admitted, but he escorted me through underbrush to what he thought was the crossing. The corner of a plowed field across the road would have been the camp site. Both sites looked authentic enough for me. Of course we chatted about life I general as we walked. He had been a rodeo rider for a few years. He remembered getting lost in Santa Fe when he competed there in the annual July event. I told him that visitors to the City Different were not alone in unsuccessfully navigating the city's convoluted arteries. We bade each other goodbye, he to continue shooting tin cans in the creek, me to search out more Trail mementos.

Fort Larned is described by western trails historian Gregory Franzwa as "one of the great jewels of the National Park Service."[6] En route to this now silent "jewel" that figured so prominently on the road to Santa Fe, I stopped at the Larned city cemetery where fine ruts were visible, tight alongside a fence. A more obscure track was set in a thickly weeded field across the road. I moved on to the Santa Fe Trail Center, a supposedly fine museum, but I will not be able to judge such until I find it open. (Two years later I succeeded. One visit cannot do it justice, such is the depth of the exhibits. When I came to the collection of vehicles, I could not resist kneeling down so as to peer under the Conestoga wagonbed to see how the tree trunks—wagon spare parts—could have been lashed to the undercarriage. The system appeared to be efficient and much less complicated than my Jeep Cherokee's jack.)

Next, I drove through the state mental hospital grounds to view several related sites. As Demi and I climbed Jenkins Hill, another Trail lookout, a hospital security patrol car approached. I told the officer my purpose., which was what he assumed. He explained that the hospital superintendent usually became over-anxious when strangers wandered around the grounds, as rightly he should. With so much history located there and a rising interest in the Trail, I am sure the officer is frequently called out to check strangers roaming about.

In searching for even a smidgen of evidence of Camp Alert, Fort Larned's predecessor for a few months, and the nearby quarry which provided stone for the fort, I came across a unit of contemporary cavalrymen—National Guardsmen. What a contrast they provided to their comrades who trod this same ground some hundred and thirty years ago. The camouflage uniforms, metal helmets, mechanized transport trucks, and dark glasses held no allure for me. Perhaps a hundred years into the future, however, that perspective will change for some other Trail buff.

The approach to Fort Larned is concealed by the now heavily wooded banks of Pawnee Fork. Once across the bridge, however the grandeur and power of the stronghold began to reveal itself. Restored to a condition closely resembling the original state, I wondered what approaching Indians thought of it when it made its first appearance on the prairies in 1860. Their prior acquaintance with other structures of the white men could not have prepared them for the "designer" stone walls, smooth milled portal columns, and red brick chimneys.

The National Park Service brochure describes the Fort as the "guardian of the Santa Fe Trail," which, indeed, it was. Yet, ironically, its last important function was, the brochure continues, "to help end the usefulness of the trail it had so long protected.... In the early 1870s, as the Santa Fe Railroad pushed west from Topeka, soldiers from Fort Larned provided protection for construction workers."[7]

The Fort ceased serving as a viable military post in 1878, and in 1884 the property was sold at public auction. Writing this ending to a noble edifice evokes sadness, although I cannot explain why, for I have no emotional attachment to the U.S. military, whatever the century or mission. But, Fort Larned was not meant to die, and in 1964 the NPS acquired the property and restored the buildings to their original handsome state.

This morning a brisk wind was blowing as always on this exposed prairie. Atop a hundred foot flag pole set in the center of the parade ground, a huge American flag snapped crisply, closely emulating a rifle report. A full morning spent touring the grounds was not sufficient enough to absorb even a scintilla of the Fort's history, for, in addition to the Fort proper, there is a mile long history and nature trail along the periphery of the Fort. It passes a number of building sites—"lost structures," as the trail guide terms them—and faint Trail ruts. In this vicinity there were actually two Trails. One fork passed south of the Fort, and it was this route that the history trail follows. The other was north of the Fort, across Pawnee Fork. The two routes joined at the southwest corner of the Fort.

Six miles southwest of the Fort a distinct collection of ruts have been preserved as part of the Fort complex. After viewing these ruts from a lookout platform, I walked the full length of the fenced-in trace. At the edge were a group of dark depressions—buffalo wallows. I would like to believe that I was able to identify them because Walt Sharp back at Chase, Kansas had instructed me in their characteristics.

My route to Dodge City again carried me across dirt roads, all which were in good condition. More ruts, Coon Creek Crossing, more DAR markers, Coronado Cross, and Fort Dodge, now a retired soldiers home. This is a community of neat little nineteenth century style structures, although only a few date back to the original Fort. When I returned to the Fort four years later, a self-guiding tour and fine interpretive markers had been installed that told the story of this historic installation. The project was made possible by the generosity of Dodge City/Ford County Development Corp, 1st National Bank of Dodge City, and the Women's Chamber of Commerce.

Eight miles east of Fort Dodge was the first of three major crossings of the Arkansas River, these being the turnoffs to the dry Cimarron Cutoff. This one was the Lower Crossing near Ford, Kansas, which was used in the early Trail period. I was following Franzwa's guide at this point, which does not always present clear written directions. I assumed Black Pool was nearby, so I crossed the river to search for it. No luck, but it gave me an opportunity to view the flowing river which caused such trouble for wagon trains in the crossing because of its depth. W.B. Napton, a Missourian who went West for health reasons, wrote that the greater part of a day was spent in gaining the south bank when he made the journey in 1857. My knowledge of draft animals was expanded by his memoirs. He claimed that oxen and mules will not pull if their bodies touch water. Mules will go to the extreme of falling down and then drown by becoming entangled in their harnesses. Fortunately, such did not occur when Napton's train crossed.

The next day the caravan rested. Perhaps it was due as much to their successful crossing as the fact that it was the 4th of July. Whichever, they celebrated by firing a few shots from assorted weapons—and the cook baked gooseberry pies.[8]

One month earlier the sad death of Kate Kingsbury occurred at this site, as Jane Elder and David Weber reported in *Trading in Santa Fe*. She was returning to her home in Santa Fe after spending a year with her family in Salem, Massachusetts. Suffering from both tuberculosis and depression, it is not certain which affliction brought on her early death. Most likely, both. Kate's body continued the journey to Santa Fe where she was buried on June 18, 1857. I have visited her grave in a most neglected cemetery. Her gravestone has faired little better, but the inscription is still legible, and the grave is in the protection and shelter of several scraggy trees and shrubs. And, yes, I have taken flowers to her.

Later, upon reading Franzwa's description of Black Pool, I realized it was on the north side of the river, a short distance off the gravel road I had followed from Fort Larned. Four years later when I was again in the area I made another attempt. I located the weedy track, but a padlocked gate prevented access to the mysterious pool. Darkness was descending and I was already late for an appointment in Larned, thus I could not search out the property owner. The next time I am in the area I must plan better. Along most of the major route between Larned and Dodge City a new sight and odor engulfed me— cattle feedlots, which over recent decades have replaced their gigantic counterparts in Kansas City and Chicago. It did not please me to see these barbaric, mucky enclosures packed with cattle awaiting their last ride to some distant slaughterhouse. To add insult to that injury, a "scenic" overlook park east of Dodge City, complete with interpretive marker, looks out, not toward the majestic prairie, but upon a huge feedlot which stretches for miles in all directions. I could not appreciate any aspect of this new cattle management concept, and quickly moved on.

By the time I reached Dodge City, I realized that time constraints would force me to abandon the next leg of the journey, that being to the head of the Cimarron Cutoff at Lakin, Kansas, but instead, proceed directly to Elkhart for the night. I did take time to drive to the unusual contemporary Plainswoman metal sculpture on the campus of Dodge City Community College. Here Demi and I were able to stretch our legs and walk on the cool green grassy mall where the art piece rests. Though totally different, it is a fitting companion to the four traditional Madonna of the Trail monuments located elsewhere on the Trail. The two contrasting styles give the Trail a timeless quality, and reinforce Marc Simmons' now immortal words, "the Santa Fe Trail lives on."

The highway between Dodge City and Elkhart is not distinguishable in any way aside from the fact that the prairies are distinguishable in their own unique way. But it was the undistinguishable that caused me some alarm. The sun was before me and low on the western horizon, making it difficult to clearly see approaching traffic. As a huge vehicle approached, I realized it was a wheat combine, and that part of the thresher extended into my lane. Fortunately, I saw it far enough in advance to swerve onto the grassy shoulder, and fortunately there was a shoulder to swerve on to. Light on the prairies can create strange apparitions or, as in this case, almost blot them from sight.

Such is the stuff of which mirages are made. Few travelers had experienced them prior to their first crossing of the prairies. Alexander Majors was totally dumbfounded when he saw what he thought was a gigantic bison bull only to discover upon walking some eighty yards toward it that it was but a small coyote. At another time he was convinced he saw "beautiful clear lakes of water, apparently not more than a mile away, with all the surroundings in the way of bulrushes and other water vegetation common to the margin of lakes."[9]

How often men were reduced to panic racing toward those illusory cruel hoaxes of hallucination we will never know. The Trail was filled with a wild assortment of demons.

Early the next morning I picked up the Cimarron Cutoff in the extreme southwest corner of Kansas and headed for Middle Spring and Point of Rocks. Would those good dirt roads I had been traveling throughout Kansas persist, or was I now too close to New Mexico where I could count on "kidney jerkers"? Each mile down the narrow road to the spring I marveled that my luck was holding. At the spring site I hiked to a circle of trees, thick brush, and tall grass, singing all the way as had been my habit where dense verdant vegetation might conceal unwelcome wild and unfriendly residents. Good sense told me not to break through that green wall (Demi could not even be coaxed to leave the car) for a glimpse of the cool spring that refreshed so many travelers at the end of the Jornada, the Spanish name given to the dangerous and dry first leg of the Cimarron Cutoff. Thus, I never saw the spring.

Farther down the road I came upon excellent ruts as they followed alongside the Cimarron River. So, I took a walk. Walking trail ruts had become as exhilarating to me as mountain hiking. The next stop was the overlook atop Point of Rocks. A long green ribbon of cottonwood trees on the plains below marked the Cimarron River. This tree-cover is very deceptive, presupposing the existence of water. Not so for most of the year, although it is always there in sand beds a few feet below the surface. But, to the naked eye the riverbed is as dry as the desert the caravans had been plodding across for sixty miles. When Josiah Gregg passed this way in 1831 he admitted that even the most experienced traders in the train were unaware they were on the banks of the river.[10]

An interpretive marker at the overlook tells the story of Point of Rocks and the river below. Here, much to my surprise, a retired couple also had sought out this remote spot. Their principal mission was to locate wildfowl, but as I described my experiences along the Trail, their interest was noticeably aroused. Their home is the open road aboard their RV. Maybe I will encounter them again in the future, somewhere along the Santa Fe Trail.

McNees Crossing, in the far northeast corner of New Mexico, was to be my next goal, but when I filled the gas tank at Boise City, Oklahoma, I discovered the coolant reservoir was extremely low and sludge-encrusted. Something was wrong to so deplete the reservoir in under five hundred miles. It was Sunday, and, of course, no mechanic was on duty in this small town. My only choice was to try to make the forty miles to Clayton, New Mexico where my luck might be better. McNees Crossing and the other sites in the loop had to be scrubbed. Wonder of wonders, I located a mechanic in Clayton. The problem mystified him. He flushed the reservoir, filled it, and I was on my way again, still a bit troubled, but willing to gamble and continue my search of the Santa Fe Trail.

Before leaving home when I was outlining the route I would follow, I had decided to bypass the New Mexico Point of Rocks because of limited time and bad roads. Now I could reconsider. It was still early afternoon. Would the ten miles of dried mud to the site be navigable for my station wagon? There was only one way to find out. Well, it was not up to Kansas standards, but not down to Santa Fe's. This rock outcropping literally was Pete and Faye Gaines' backyard.

A very noisy dog signaled our arrival at the ranch house. A lady emerged from the house to reassure me it was safe to leave my car and walk to the base of the Rock. I roamed around, gazing at the rugged protrusion and at the ground which was strewn with rocks. Some were even gathered in small piles, and I wondered if these could be some of the eleven known, but unmarked, graves of travelers who died within the shadows of Point of Rocks. Then I turned 180 degrees to view the broad, level plain beyond the house. Yes, ruts could easily be seen from this distance as they cut a long swath through what is now rangeland.

What a cavalcade of history was played out on the sweeping

terrain around me, much which was violent, as attested to by the graves of those eleven people at the base of the Point. The records of persons who passed this way indicate that there were many more whose final resting places are known only to God. Following the Mexican War, violence at the Point escalated significantly. Time and again caravans were ambushed by Indians who found the mesa an excellent hiding spot. Today those rocks provide an excellent platform to view the Gaines' ranch buildings, cattle, the lush canyon through which flows the waters of the springs issuing from cracks in the Rocks, and the broad prairie that gathers all to its abundant bosom.

Note: Two years later on July 26, 1992 I visited Point of Rocks at the certification of the site by the NPS. What a gala event it was. Over 200 people determined that the monsoon rains that had pelted northeastern New Mexico for several weeks would not deter them from driving that forbidding road to the Gaines ranch. It was at the barbeque picnic in the canyon that I first met Paul Bentrup. I will only say that he is unforgettable. Oh yes, his knowledge of the Santa Fe Trail is legendary, and he admires Bulldogs. Although we all knew our purpose for being there was to witness certification of the site, it was the dedication of a replica of Isaac Allen's grave marker (Isaac's grave is the only resting spot at the Point that was originally marked, so far as is known) that moved me most, specifically, the tender tribute Harry Myers spoke to Isaac. Harry said:

Hello Isaac Allen,

I imagine that no one has spoken to you in about a hundred years, maybe longer. We are here on a special day today, a day which we honor those like you who took part in a great adventure. And we also mark the placing of your new gravestone.

We know your name, Isaac. We know the date of your death. But we don't know anything else.

Who were you? And what was your role in this great adventure?

Were you a farm boy from Missouri whose imagination was captured by the news of the Mexican War and ran off to participate? Or were you already a teamster, a herder, or a wagonmaster who was seasoned in the rigors of the trail?

Had you already been to Santa Fe, or were you eagerly anticipating time in the fabled city when you met your death?

And how did you die? Did you die peacefully of disease or sickness in the cool prairie evening or did you die a violent death in the hot afternoon sun? Lewis Garrard said: "To die anywhere seems hard, but to heave the last breath...on the burning, desolate prairie...[seems] hard indeed." But I think not, buried here in 1848 in this magnificent prairie, this cathedral of New Mexico.

That year, Isaac, 1848, was a year of people crossing the Santa Fe Trail back and forth. We know that by mid-July, 1848 over 3,000 Government and Traders wagons and 12,000 people had passed Fort Mann. It was the year that the Mexican War ended, but because news traveled slow, there were still recruits for the War coming down the trail. And in August of that year going back up the trail along with the veterans who had served in Mexico and New Mexico. But we know you weren't a soldier, Isaac, you aren't mentioned in any of the muster rolls.

But we do know that in the same year of your death, Sergeant John Story of the Illinois Volunteers died here exactly one month short of 144 years ago, on August 26, 1848. Did you die before or after him?

Were the remains of Mr. White's party, who were killed the next year in 1849, interred here? If so, your grave is joined by that of a black woman, an Indian, and two Hispanic New Mexicans, along with several Anglo-Americans

You were well thought of, Isaac. Finding a suitable stone and carving your name in it took not only some effort, but some time as well. For some, a wooden cross sufficed. For some, just burial in an unmarked grave was enough. But, your companions marked your resting place for all who passed, to know that at this landmark, you lie in rest.

And your rest has not been peaceful, Isaac. We know that at least once your grave, as have all the others, has been dug into. How many other times has greed and blind stupidity disturbed your sacred rest?

There is so little that we know about you, Isaac, and so much that we do not know. But, perhaps that is good, for you serve as a representative of all those who passed each way on this trail. You were the spirit of two nations bound together by a tiny trail on this huge continent. You were the Missouri farm boy who longs for adventure, the seasoned teamster whose trips were now second nature, the wagon owner-entrepreneur out to make a fortune in new and strange lands. You were the raw recruit who sickened and died on the way to Santa Fe, or the grizzled veteran who died just before home and your loved ones.

And you are the spirit of this great trail and the spirit of all those who walked every foot of this trail and thereby joined two nations in an adventure that touches us today.

You are the spirit of the past, Isaac. And you are the spirit of the future, Isaac, for only in knowing of your sacrifice and the sacrifice of your fellow-travelers on the trail, can we learn how to be citizens of our nation today, and maintain the greatness that you helped us to achieve in this wonderful adventure, The Santa Fe Trail!

Rest in honor and dignity now, Isaac. For you are of us, and we of you.

The crowd ringing Isaac's grave stood in respectful silence, not wanting to break the spell of that tender monologue. But Faye quietly informed us that we would have just enough time to beat the rain that was rapidly approaching. So the crowd quickly dispersed to their autos. My driver, Woody Taylor, wanted to stop at the historic Dorsey Mansion, five miles farther down the bumpy gravel road, hoping we could stay ahead of the coming storm. Unfortunately, a torrent hit as we were touring the mansion. Well, the damage was done, and we could only hope that Woody's trusty VW that was our "Rockaway carriage" could successfully navigate fifteen miles of "muckety muck" to Highway 56. Often we became stuck, but always managed to break free from the muck. Behind us were six or seven other vehicles engaged in the same struggle as we. The only difference, being in the lead we did not have to plow through the mucky ruts that quickly became the road. One hour and more later, we reached solid pavement, and for many miles thereafter mud flung in all directions from our incrusted vehicle. Squeaky Clean car wash benefited greatly from that excursion to Point of Rocks.

How long I strolled this famous spot back on that Sunday in 1990, gazing in one direction then another, I do not know. It was too beautiful to abandon quickly, and the mental image had to remain with me for a long time. Could not the same be said for all I had viewed these last three days? Maybe I should resurrect my camera from the drawer where it has lain idle for six years so that I can recall these scenes at will.

I slowly drove away, parting several cows who were reclining on the road and did not wish to be disturbed. Time and again I stopped to either look back at the awesome landmark or walk a few yards down more ruts. Being a rock hound, I picked up a rock—common-looking by most standards, but meaningful to me. It has taken its place beside Marion Russell's rock on my patio.

The remainder of the drive home followed old familiar Trail sites. Wagon Mound resembles a covered wagon more strikingly each time I pass it. This time I tried to bring sharper form to the lower mound on the right which is said to resemble a pair of oxen. The eight miles of ruts paralleling the Interstate as it approaches the Fort Union exit were exceptionally vivid against the late afternoon sun. Watrous, Tiptonville, Sapello Stage Station, Tecolote, San Miguel, Pecos National Historic Park, and more passed in quick succession.

This highly scenic stretch of the Trail has impressed many other travelers, both current and past. Lydia Spencer Lane, an Army wife in the mid nineteenth century, wrote about this road in her memoir, *I Married a Soldier.* Her husband was commander of Fort Union, and oftentimes she made the hundred and eighty mile eight-day round trip between the Fort and Santa Fe. She found the drive "delightful," with the scenery beautiful and at times even "grand". "The breeze," she wrote, "filled with the odor of pine-trees, was exhilarating and delicious—you seemed to take in health with every breath of the pure air."[11] Well said, Lydia.

As I read Lydia's words, I catch a whiff of those conifers, and those scenic mountains are imprinted in memory. On this particular day I write about, the beautiful scenery was spread before me, but I had to be content to let my mind's eye retrieve from memory those special Trail sites that I had wandered before. Just knowing they are there and being preserved, in many instances, is comforting.

When the dim shadow of the Sangre de Cristo mountains were replaced by precise contours and shapes, I knew I was home. What a special meaning that holds for me. I did not start singing "there is no place like home," but I knew that for me home is in New Mexico beside the Santa Fe Trail, and there is nowhere else on earth I would rather be. The sight of my little adobe with its much too neat landscaping loomed around the corner. Ah yes, how good it was to be home. Yet it would not require much persuasion to hit the Trail again—tomorrow morning, perhaps?

Dare I compare my feelings with those of Lydia Lane when she exclaimed, "[t]here was certainly something fascinating in the roving life we led that exactly suited me."[12]

Notes

1. Gregg, Josiah. *The Commerce of the Prairies.* Milo Milton Quaife (Ed.). Lincoln, Nebraska: University of Nebraska Press, 1967, p. 44.

2. Schulz, Ray S. Murder, Massacre, and Misfortune Near Walnut Creek Crossing. In Leo E. Oliva (Ed.) *Confrontation on the Santa Fe Trail.* Larned, Kansas: Santa Fe Trail Association, 1996, pgs. 100-103.

3. Trail Letter by Michael Speck, 1852. In Marc Simmons (Ed.) *On the Santa Fe Trail.* Lawrence, Kansas: University Press of Kansas, 1986, p. 24.

4. Gregg, *op. cit., p.* 49, n.29

5. Drumm, Stella M. (Ed.). *Down the Santa Fe Trail and Into Mexico: The Diary of Susan Shelby Magoffin, 1846–1847.* Lincoln, Nebraska: University of Nebraska Press, 1982, p. 40.

6. Franzwa, Gregory. *The Santa Fe Trail Revisited.* St. Louis, Missouri: The Patrice Press, 1989, p. 114.

7. Fort Larned. National Park Service, Interpretive brochure, 1987.

8. Napton, W. B. *Over the Santa Fe Trail in 1857.* Arrow Rock, Missouri: Friends of Arrow Rock, 1991, pgs. 33-34.

9. Majors, Alexander. *Seventy Years on the Frontier.* Lincoln, Nebraska: University of Nebraska Press, 1989, p. 157.

10. Gregg, *op. cit.,* p. 66.

11. Lane, Lydia Spencer. *I Married a Soldier.* Albuquerque, New Mexico: University of New Mexico Press, 1987, 147.

12. *Ibid.,* 137.

New Mexico Point of Rocks certification ceremony.

Isaac Allen's grave, New Mexico Point of Rocks.

3

Trail Memories from Eastern Kansas

A friend (Wanda Lathom) was being married in Kansas City in October of 1991, and that was all the incentive I needed to again go Trail-trekking. This venture would cover eastern Kansas plus a few specially selected Kansas City sites. My hosts in Kansas City would be my former University of Kansas roommate, Nogah Silberman, husband Mel, and daughter Carol. Because since time immemorial our visits have been giant talkathons, I wondered if I could entice them to join me on a tour of those city sites I had selected. No problem, for they were eager to learn more about the Santa Fe Trail. So, off we went in their twentieth century wagon, i.e., Lincoln Towncar, to Westport, the location of Kansas City's origin, where so much Trail history was rooted.

Since it was time to "noon," what better place to begin our tour than at Stanford and Sons restaurant. The building was built in 1850 by Cyprian Chouteau, younger brother of Auguste Chouteau of Chouteau's Island fame. The island was located in the Arkansas River in southwest Kansas. However, it no longer exists because numerous meanderings of the river have left it landlocked south of the present channel. The building, which housed a store and warehouse, was sold sixteen years later to Jim Bridger, whose name symbolizes all the romance and daring embodied in the western movement and the mountain men who created it. Although the present edifice has maintained its historical integrity, there was no hint of the Trail in the bill of fare. Making no attempt to even mask a typical Trail feast of beans, bread, salt pork, and an occasional apple, I settled on a mushroom quiche and green salad.

Following lunch we strolled through Westport which, to some

degree, has attempted to recapture its halcyon days, although the trendiness shows through. From one site to the next we moved, with me reading all the while from Simmons' guidebook. At a tiny triangular park sandwiched between noisy thoroughfares, we paused beside a magnificent bronze sculpture created by Tom Beard commemorating three Westport giants—Alexander Majors, who with partners Russell and Waddell operated one of the largest freighting firms along the western trails; John Calvin McCoy, who platted Westport; and previously acknowledged Jim Bridger. We all circled the larger than life monument exclaiming over the precise detail of hands, waistcoat buttons, powder pouch, and much more. Reluctantly, we moved on to interpretive markers, the exact number which I quickly lost an accounting of. There was the stunning relocated Harris House, the private residence of the operator of the now demised Harris House Hotel. That hotel was the last roof to cover the heads of many Trail travelers until they reached Santa Fe. The Westport Historical Society, present owner of the house, has restored several rooms which are open most days to the public. Unfortunately, this was not one of those days. At a freight wagon displayed in another tiny park, the narrow width of the wagon box prompted a lively discussion among us as to its authenticity.

By now the Silberman's interest in the Trail was at fever pitch, so we added Penn Valley Park to the itinerary. Because it is no longer safe to stroll this park even in broad daylight, Mel discouraged us from leaving the car to more closely examine the fine statuary displayed there. However, when I saw the massive Pioneer Mother bronze sculpture, I remarked that I must get a closer look, the risk notwithstanding. Nogah and I quickly walked to the brow of a hill which supported the art piece. I was quickly overpowered, not by a mugger, but by the beauty of this woman on horseback cradling an infant and protected by two grizzled-appearing foot "soldiers". Whatever romantic notions the mind conjures up about the westward movement was quickly dispelled as I viewed the disheveled clothing, facial wrinkles, matted beards, and gaunt pony. The uncommon artistry of the sculptor left no doubt that the pioneer's life was, indeed, hard and frightening—and there was no symphony orchestra providing background music as the train trudged along toward the far horizon.

The next morning Nogah and I headed for Minor Park to view the most dramatic collection of ruts in Kansas City. I quickly located four swales, the deepest which straddled a DAR marker. As we walked the full length there were sections where our eyes could not see beyond its rim. At moments such as these, I always find it hard to breathe, notice my quickened heart-beat, feel my eyes starring unswervingly down the narrow trace, and no longer hear the sounds about me. This may sound over-dramatic to anyone who has not come under the spell of the Santa Fe trail and, perhaps, even to some who have. Be that as it may, this is how I experience the Trail.

Several historic homes were on my list that day, the first being Alexander Majors' fine antebellum residence. Realizing how many excellent period houses in this country have fallen to a wrecking crew, my congratulations and thanks go out to the Alexander Majors Historical Trust for its unswerving preservation efforts. Our tour guide led us out to the front second floor balcony, pointing out that the busy thoroughfare and compact residential area directly before us once held the many oxen, mules, wagons, and maintenance structures required for this mega-freighting operation.

Majors claimed in his memoirs that he decided to enter the freighting business because farming did not produce sufficient income to support his growing family. He wrote, "As I was brought up to handle animals and had been employed more or less in the teaming business, after looking the situation over, it occurred to me there was nothing I was so well adapted for...as the freighting business...between Independence...and Santa Fe...."[1]

As naïve as this sounds, that decision led to the outfitting of six wagons, and on August 10, 1848 Majors modestly entered the freighting business. Larger business operation enterprises have had as modest beginnings, yet the realization that "the American dream" exists continues to amaze me. Later, with partners William H. Russell and William B. Waddell, they expanded to encompass the entire west and organized the famed Pony Express. It is to Alexander Majors that Kansas City owes its very existence, and the growth and prosperity which ultimately propelled it to the status it holds today as a major American city.

We moved on to the Seth Ward house, but it was not this beautiful edifice that lured me so much as the small house behind it which for a time was owned by William Bent. Both are private residences, and because no one responded to my knock at the Ward house, I had to be content to catch just a veiled glimpse of the Bent house, for it was surrounded by heavy foliage. Maybe I will be more fortunate another time. (And so I was, which will be covered elsewhere.)

The following morning I sadly bade the Silbermans farewell and again hit the Trail, with a DAR marker in Overland Park, Kansas as my first stop. For the next two hours I leapfrogged from one landmark to the next. My bad luck at not finding places opened followed me to the Mahaffie house and barn, circa 1865, which had been a stage station and caravan overnight stop. But, I was able to stroll the grounds around this handsome two-story native stone house and get a feel for what might have transpired there as the heavy trail traffic rumbled by.

My own experience with traffic occurred trying to get to U.S. 56 in the Olathe area, which was compounded by highway construction detours. After several unsuccessful attempts to locate a DAR marker and campground, I had to admit defeat and move on. Strange as it may seem, that even without highway signs or maps, and even in the face of uncharted territory and few landmarks to guide the travelers along the nine hundred mile route, fewer people became lost in the Trail's full sixty year existence than probably occurs in a single day in present-day Kansas City.

When I pulled onto the grounds of the old Lanesfield school, now a museum, imagine my surprise not only to find it open but to see children playing in the yard. The "school marm," dressed in period costume, informed me that the children from a local consolidated school were on a day long field trip at the old school. I strolled through the classroom. There were the all too familiar portraits from my own school days of Lincoln and Washington watching over the old style desks on which were placed little ink wells with companion pens. The open penmanship books were filled with those connecting ovals/circles which extended unbroken from left to right edges of the page. I wondered if those drills truly dated back to 1869 when the school was built.

Back in the schoolyard I asked the "school marm," an employee of this Johnson County Museum, if the ruts that intersected the grounds mentioned by Franzwa were visible. Much to my surprise, she firmly declared that there were no ruts here or anywhere else in Johnson County. Her knowledge of the Trail is apparently scanty, for, indeed, there are ruts in Johnson County, some which are as fine as anywhere along the Trail's nine hundred mile length. For example, an excellent hundred and eight foot long swale exists in Overland Park's Harmon Park, a site that has been certified by the NPS. Incidentally, the Silbermans and I visited the park in 1992. The park sits on a high hill, which it shares with a water tower. Even though this was a heavily urbanized area, I was able to mentally strip away all those buildings and the water tower and imagine what this view was like to the travelers who were heading west for a great adventure over a hundred and fifty years ago. NPS has constructed a shelter with interpretive markers that present a compelling story. A concrete path leads to the swale. I would have preferred gravel, for a natural medium would have created a more authentic feel.

A few miles farther down the road from the Lanesfield School brought me to Black Jack Park on the eastern edge of Baldwin City. Although Baldwin City is not formally declared a Trail complex, the number of sites in its vicinity certainly qualifies it for such distinction. Across from the Park, which gained its fame from a battle fought in 1858 between pro-slavery and abolitionist forces, the latter led by John Brown, a gentle rise, generously spread with tall grasses and weeds, concealed excellent ruts. This is the Ivan Boyd Prairie Preserve—18 acres of virgin prairie. How Lilliputian this patch is when compared with the original historic prairie lands which covered a ninth of the North American continent—from Illinois west to the feet of the Rocky Mountains and south Texas north to central Alberta, Canada. As I began my walk up a narrow footpath, the ruts gradually revealed themselves, first up the path I traversed, then to both left and right. Cresting the hill and turning to face the route I had just trod, there they were, as distinct as though free of the heavy growth. In fact, the growth itself revealed the contour of the road by its more pronounced color against the vegetation around it.

A few steps farther and I came upon a crude monument that looked as though it had been freshly dug from the area and rolled to its present site. Hard as I tried, I could not decipher the time-worn inscription save for the identification—"Sibley Survey 1825." The U.S. Congress authorized that the Trail be properly surveyed, and this marker indicated that the survey team was on the job in Baldwin City. However, the marker dates back only to the 1940s, and I have found no record of any original surviving markers. It is hardly any wonder, since Sibley's party marked the route with sod mounds which quickly succumbed to erosion, stampeding buffalo herds, or a trail version of vandalism. The next stop was "the Castle," Baldwin's fine circa 1858 stone museum—closed.

The town boasted numerous historical markers commemorating its colorful past, more ruts (some vivid, others more imagined than genuine), a well, sites of ancient structures (also better imagined than visible), and the ever-present sense of blurring between past and present.

It was well past "nooning," which I chose to partake of inside my Cherokee by the side of a dusty road rather than combat the gale-force winds, the true trademark of the prairies. Yet I was only a scant 40 miles west of my starting point that morning. The thought of where I would spend the night crept into consciousness. My route did not hold great promise, and I did not want to take any detour to find a town large enough to boast a motel. I would not think about that now; I would think about it later. Now I wanted to focus totally on the terrain that spread before me, imagining I could see the oxen that had broken from Susan Magoffin's camp in this vicinity as they mounted a ridge and headed back for Missouri.[2]

On the northwest edge of Baldwin City is a small park containing a DAR and two Santa Fe Trail historical markers. It is a very modest plot, which has been left in its natural state. The only grooming appears to be an occasional mowing. I found this to be a most appropriate "design" for a park set out to commemorate the nineteenth century movement. Continuing beyond the park about a half-mile, I came upon a pasture containing distinct ruts. As I gazed at the trace, I sighed and slowly shook my head. Lawrence, where I lived for over fifteen years, was a short fifteen miles north. Had I been interested in the Trail in those days I could have visited all that I had seen today plus much more to come many times without the time and distance constraints that faced me now. Fifteen miles then as against seven hundred and fifty miles now.

Note: Over the years I had returned to this area, but not until 2009 did several significant sites produce the need to revisit them. That year, 2009, the SFTA symposium was held in Arrow Rock, Missouri. Again, Faye Gaines was my passenger, and again we were traveling through country new to her. Gardner, Kansas, where the Santa Fe Trail and the Oregon-California Trail parted, boasted a new interpretive site which had recently been completed through the partnership of SFTA and the NPS. I had only seen photos of the site, and these did not engage me—too gentrified, in my view. However, I was most pleased upon arrival to see that the site was almost as natural as in the trail days. The small roofed shelter which housed the interpretive panels was "architecturally" appropriate. Several low stone walls intermittently located along the concrete path were not as gentrified as the photos indicated. The native grasses were allowed to grow to their natural height and density, and had not been mowed. John Atkinson, SFTA director of the project, did an excellent job of bringing the history of the site alive to all those who stop by, and many do just that rather than drive on down the road.

Nearby Lanesfield school was our next destination. My memory of its location from my first visit failed me, and we wound around back roads longer than I thought we should. Directional signage was not the best. A new visitors center had been built since my last visit. The curator filled in some historical gaps from my earlier visit. For example, the school was named for James Lane, a powerful and controversial figure during Kansas' struggle for statehood during the period known as "Bleeding Kansas," the days leading up to the Civil War. Some historians convincingly, in my view, argue that those turbulent days were actually the opening shots of that horrible war that historian Shelby Foote claims "defined the U.S. as a nation."

These "Bleeding Kansas" days were noted by at least one Trail traveler, James Larkin, a St. Louis citizen who went west seeking health. He wrote, "Today we passed in sight of Lawrence.... Within past 2 days we have passed houses uninhabited on account of the Kansas difficulties, & some that have been burned. One was burning as we passed. Almost every one living on the road has been plundered, robbed or driven away by one side or the other—Missourians or Freesoilers. The country is in an awful condition...."[3]

The visitor center curator was unaware of the precise location of ruts behind the school, but at least, he did not deny their existence, as did the "teacher" I encountered during my previous visit.

On our return from Arrow Rock we checked out the next sites down the road, these being new to Faye, but repeats for me—Baldwin City, which is west of Gardner. First stop was Black Jack Park. The park continues to be well cared for, and the modest interpretive sign boards tell the story of the battle fought here in 1858. Across from the park are excellent ruts. Being late September, the grasses had grown quite tall, but we were just able to identify the four, and sometimes five, distinct parallel ruts coursing westward. Unfortunately, we did not explore farther in the dense vegetation for the supposed Sibley survey marker. Then into a significantly developed Baldwin City we drove. No longer is this a tiny town, but rather a sizable bedroom community to Kansas City. We drove by the Santa Fe well, Palmyra town site marker, and the Trail park.

I will pick up the next leg of this journey when we approach Durham.

Returning to 1991, just west of Globe, but a few miles west of Baldwin City, stood what once was a large dressed-limestone house on the side of a hill, now only a fading memory. The state of dilapidation belied its former magnificence as the Simmons Point stage station. I walked up to the edge of a rubble-and-weed-strewn yard for a closer look. Perched high above the ground at the second floor level was the cornerstone with the year 1870 engraved indelibly on it. Why was this commemorative marker not at ground level where it belonged? An interesting question which I am unable to answer. Because the Trailhead had moved west by that year, some Trail authorities question any connection with the house. Some years later I stopped again at the house en route to Lawrence, but strangely could not find the cornerstone.

At Overbrook, five miles farther west, I searched out the cemetery. Yes, indeed, the Trail coursed right through that quiet retreat, just as it does in so many other final resting places between Old Franklin and Santa Fe. A post at the back of the cemetery had been placed in the middle of a rut. No markings on the stone explained if it was set in this spot to identify the Trail. It is a boon to Trail buffs that the standard death ritual in America is burial in the ground which is set aside specifically for this purpose, and now often preserves Trail ruts where otherwise the ground would have been plowed up or developed.

Although I stopped at each site listed in my guidebook, I was not able to locate all of them or else could not identify what I saw. Should I accept what I saw—or didn't see? Such is not that easy because a big part of the adventure is to mentally strip away the intervening years between the present and the Trail era. However, when a site does not immediately reveal itself, that journey back in time contains a void, perhaps akin to what an amnesiac experiences when he or she is confronted with an absence of "past." More often than not, it compels me to want to return at a later time when I may discover that the slate has now been filled. Of course, return trips all along the Trail are a foregone conclusion in order to visit all those museums that I have found closed.

Late that day I pulled off the road, walked through a thicket, down a gentle bank, and into the middle of 110 Mile Creek. Here I was at yet another location filled with so much Trail lore. While camped here, Susan Magoffin spoke passionately of the freedom and vitality she felt. W.W.H. Davis also spoke passionately about his experiences at the Creek, but his emotions were born out of witnessing a prairie fire that lit up the night skies almost to the brightness of day. Had the winds shifted, however, he might not have survived to write this almost romantic description of the conflagration. "The blaze...licked up the dry grass like so much gossamer, and cracked like the reports of a thousand pistols as the flames ran along with the wind.... It assumed various forms. Sometimes it shot several feet into the air, like the forked tongue of a serpent; the next moment it would almost disappear, as an opposite breath of wind would arrest its progress; then it starts again into new life, with its fiery tongue licking up every living thing within reach."[4]

Viewing the bush-studded banks and the giant trees towering over all, I sensed my own tranquil mood perhaps akin to that Susan felt. That such an idyllic spot could be given such a prosaic name as "110 Mile Creek" can only be charged to the unromantic nature of engineers in the Sibley survey; well, maybe their practicality. The Creek is a hundred and ten miles from Fort Osage, Missouri, mile zero on the survey route. But, where was the water? Nary a patch of mud could be found beneath my feet. I followed the watercourse in both directions, finally detecting a small silver pool as the Creek made a northerly bend. This tiny puddle notwithstanding, I knew that the photo I took would beg explanation.

A mile up the highway I turned onto a deeply rutted track road. I am sure my Cherokee was purring gleefully as we bounced along, and I could almost hear her say, "It's about time I had a little fun doing what I enjoy best." At the end of the road stood the remains of the McGee-Harris stage station. All four of the stone and frame walls remained upright to some degree or other, I noted with surprise. Yet another structure was hidden among dense foliage some yards away, and Simmons claims there were even more buildings when the enterprise was active between 1854 and 1866. What a surprise this tiny community must have been to the travelers who had seen no habitation for days. Set in a lovely meadow that sloped down to meet tree-lined 110 Mile Creek, I audibly sighed at the beauty around. Yes, this was another exceptional place to be tucked in memory forever.

Ten miles west I entered Burlingame, the town which boasts its main street to be the Santa Fe Trail. As I glanced from one building to the next, many which dated back to Trail days, I wondered what tales these silent guards of the Trail held within their walls. Did they yearn for the sight of the lumbering oxen pulling such strange looking chariots of the prairie, or is it today's chariots from Detroit that are the strange ones?

Just west of town was another stage station—Havanna— bearing the name of a long- abandoned community. As I drove down the heavily overgrown path that easily concealed my vehicle, I know I heard my Cherokee giggle as the foliage tickled its underside. Not until I was within a few feet of the station was its presence revealed. The native limestone structure, like the McGee-Harris buildings, was quite well preserved. Because of all those weeds, I did not see the approaching pickup truck until it had pulled up beside my car. Thinking the driver would reprimand me for trespassing on private property, I jovially greeted him and stated my purpose. No, he did not wish to evict me; yes, he knew the history of the building. The local SFTA chapter was searching for some way to lease the acreage surrounding the station, and would I be interested in acquiring it. Admittedly, the thought did not fall on fallow ground, but that is another story, and a financially absurd one at best. We continued to chat about the Trail, farming, and Kansas. Again I had encountered one of the good Kansas folk.

The day was quickly waning, so I inquired where I might find lodging. Much to my delight, he informed me that there was a motel in Osage City, the next town on my westerly route. No need to detour to Topeka, although returning to one of my former homes was tempting. Before heading south for Osage City, I drove a quarter of a mile farther west on U.S. 56 to the grave of Private Samuel Hunt who died on the Trail in 1835. Marked graves were not common, thus the Private's final resting place is special, so much so that a modern tombstone was erected some hundred years later. In Osage City I acquired more friends—a delightful Beagle, whom I took for a walk, and a passel of cats I decided were her stepbrothers and sisters.

Excitement mounted as I hit the road the next morning. This day I would be in Council Grove, the very name that shouts Santa Fe Trail. But first I would experience the beauty of the Flint Hills, the home of the famous Bluestem tallgrass—six million acres of grass-covered prairie, so high that it can conceal a man on horseback.

The highway cut a dull charcoal swath through the gently rolling hills. It was October, so they wore their soft rust tinted robe. It was as though God, from above, spread out a gigantic velvet blanket, let it slip from his/her fingers, and float gently to earth. Having driven through these Flint Hills many times during the twenty-two years Kansas was my home and since, I marvel that each time, I am gripped by their simple beauty as though I am viewing them for the first time.

Yet this beauty, about which I can soliloquize unendingly escapes many travelers. A Californian, so the story goes, passed a sign on the Kansas Turnpike announcing, "Scenic Overlook ahead." "Only in Kansas," he snickered, "is it necessary to announce that one is in a scenic area." I would encourage that Californian and readers of the present work to read W.W.H. Davis' description of the prairie,[5] it being too lengthy to quote here. The prairies are more an internal or perhaps an introspective experience than external. All too many people, including many of my friends, believe Kansas is to be gotten "through" rather than "to." To them I would quote the hackneyed expression, "beauty is in the eye of the beholder." Whether or not these words were meant for the prairies, I cannot imagine anyone not being in awe when in the midst of the Flint Hills.

Shortly after returning home I read William Least Heat-Moon's recent bestseller, *PrairyErth*. This 624-page volume is about Chase County, Kansas, the county immediately south of my route that day, and the heart of the Flint Hills. Its seven hundred eighty square miles carries a population of a mere three thousand souls. Of course, "beautiful" is not the adjective most frequently heard when describing Chase County, thus how remarkable to find this scholarly author writing in poetic and philosophic language, expressing an effervescence that even I have not experienced.

Trail pilgrims could match Heat-Moon's eloquence, however. One can almost hear the musical bounce in Susan Magoffin's voice as she wrote, "Oh, this is a life I would not exchange for a great deal... so much free uncontaminated air."[6] (air pollution, even in 1846.); and later, on a hill above Council Grove, "to the west...as far as the eye can reach nothing but a waving sea of tall grass.... I went up onto it at sunset, and thought I had not seen, ever, a more imposing sight."[7] Words failed Lewis H. Garrard, yet he managed to project the feeling with, "a too vivid picture [of the scenery]...cannot be portrayed."[8] And the spiritual embodiment of the Trail, Marion Sloan Russell, in poetry that knows no equal, "the earth was like a Persian rug, the lavender, red and yellow wild flowers mingling with the silvery green prairie grass...and where the wild grapevines ran riot."[9]

These words and others provided a silent accompaniment

to the visual scene spread before me as I rolled toward Council Grove. Very soon I came upon the first of many stone fences that dot the countryside. Most are now mere fragments of once imposing barricades that stretched across the prairie, reaching to, and then farther west becoming lost in the tallgrass. I was quite surprised when I first encountered these fences many years ago, for they seemed so out of place in this expansive country. This was not New England, and it certainly was light-years removed from the British Isles where even today stone walls outnumber fences. Yet, in this section of Kansas, limestone is abundant as was the aversion against barbed wire, thus, when ranchers reluctantly took to fencing, stone was the material of choice.

Half expecting that the mental image of the approach to Council Grove as given to me by Trail chroniclers would be much as they had described it, I was surprised when I was at the Neosho River bridge without any advance warning. The river bisects the town, east to west. Present day Council Grove is exceedingly proud of its historical past, and has taken great effort—and money—to preserve everything. A self-guided auto tour has been laid out, complete with markers and an interpretive brochure. The Chamber of Commerce representative loaded me down with a stack of pamphlets and maps, insisting that I not bypass anything. But her mission that day was to lobby for a tallgrass prairie park. I believe that the prairie grasses should be left in private ownership, and that with the establishment of certain covenants their integrity could be better maintained than in government hands. With that history in mind, I queried her about the current legislation. As we talked I heard the Trail beckoning me, so piling the additional information about the monument on top of the other stack, I assured her I would give it my attention, thanked her for her warm hospitality, and commenced the town tour.

The Madonna of the Trail statue, one of four along the Trail, has held me spellbound since I first saw it some years ago. Slowly I circled its base, attempting to memorize every detail of the carefully chiseled form of mother and children. Upon each viewing yet another and new detail reveals itself. Still, the one most powerful particular that has been with me since first sight are her shoes—not "shoes," but high top men's work boots. Those boots deliver the message of the reality of the western pioneer movement—heavy, sturdy, marred, mud-caked, capable of bearing the wearer through all adversity. They bespeak another meaning of "femininity," and I am not so sure but that it is a meaning more accurate and abiding than all others ascribed to the "fair sex." Yet, the mark of that more universally acknowledged feminine characteristic is not missing from the madonna—a sunbonnet bearing a garland of flowers about its crown.

Insisting upon a closer view of the river, I mounted a levee and walked a few hundred yards along that modest stream, which for all caravans was transformed into a giant laundromat. Over a century plus later, the banks as far as the eye can see are once again heavily wooded, although the hardwood trees have not yet recovered from their sacrifice as spare parts for the crude wagons. But where was the actual ford? Of course, right beside the Pizza Hut.

Matt Field overflowed with exuberance as he described the descent to the river, and the "merry days we...spent in 'Council Grove.'... We sang duets, one on one side, and one on the other of the beautiful stream..."[10] fishing, swimming, singing, and joining in merrymaking with new-found friends from other caravans who had rendezvoused for the long pull through the dangerous wilderness that was before them. This is but one example of Matt's charming and effusive literary style. Was the two-month trip to Santa Fe truly that jolly? For Matt, apparently so.

At the native stone Kaw Indian Mission I found not ruins, but an elegant mansion. Following its service as a school for Indian children and later as the first for white children in Kansas, it was remodeled extensively and became the home of a leading local citizen. The docent on duty regaled me with information about all the local sites when she learned I was following the Trail. She and her husband helped organize a trail ride in 1988 and hope to repeat another soon, an activity that piques my interest.

A visit to Council Grove is not complete without lunch at the Hays House. By the time I walked in the door I was as hungry as any Trail sojourner who had eagerly anticipated the sumptuous fare served by owner Seth Hays. The present restaurant staff was not well-versed in Trail history, but I was given a pamphlet documenting the building's history and invited to browse upstairs and down. Although of modest but sturdy construction and simple decor, it must have appeared as a palace to Trailers, particularly those eastbound, for any structures at all were very few and far between from here to Santa Fe.

Although I saw all in Council Grove that related to the Trail, I could have lingered longer at each site, but I had many miles yet to travel, so I reluctantly pulled myself away, vowing to return, and soon. I made one last stop—on the west edge of town—duplicating a practice of all Trailers by calling at the Last Chance store. Here they stocked up on supplies to carry them through to Santa Fe. Hopefully, they rarely encountered what I did—it was closed.

It was now late afternoon, and I had been hopping from one site to another searching out traces of ruts, Diamond Spring, and historical markers. To reach Diamond Spring required bouncing down back gravel roads to the Diamond Spring Ranch road, then across open country that gave no hint of lush foliage that one associates with a natural water source. However, following the directions of the ranch manager's wife, the road led past the main house and ranch buildings, down a gentle grade to a shady grove. There I found a cement stock tank, which holds the water issuing from the ground. The green scum on the water's surface made it difficult to believe that this was the "Diamond of the Desert" so named by George Sibley when his 1825 Trail survey came upon it. Would Josiah Gregg, Marion Russell, Susan Magoffin, and others who marveled at the crystal clarity and sweetness of this fount recognize it today? I doubt it. Looks can be deceiving, however, for beneath that frothy surface sweet water still issues forth. Quite recently the Spring attracted Least Heat-Moon's interest even though it is in Morris County one county north of Chase. He expounded and quoted liberally about the site *per se* and the history it produced. I was surprised to learn of a number of Trail journalists previously unknown to me that his research had uncovered: Colonel John Hughes, Abraham Johnston, George Gibson, Philip Gooch Ferguson, English immigrant H.M.T. Powell (Heat-Moon believes his record is one of the best), Max Greene, Sergeant Percival Lowe, Samuel Kingman, Charles Post—all new friends to whom I am forever grateful for recording their Trail memories.

Now I was at Lost Spring. This lovely sylvan paradise features a number of small pools along a creek from which rises a watercress-shrouded spring. It was a perfect spot for a walk, so I headed out along the creek bank, watching the pools of water play hide-and-seek along the creek's course. How contrasting my experience was from that of Susan Magoffin. Here her caravan sat out the day while it rained uninterruptedly. Even her palatial tent, which usually was secured from all calamities, was awash as "water ran through [it] like a little spring, so we just turned the carpet up to the pole, and left that part of the house to see after itself"[11], observing all from her bed where she had retreated to keep her feet dry.

This secluded oasis lured me farther into its verdant cloister until, noting the waning sun on the horizon, I reluctantly retraced my steps. However, before quitting this Garden of Eden entirely, I was compelled to turn and take one last, longing gaze, embedding it indelibly in my memory, and vowing to return again, which I did on several occasions.

In Tampa—Kansas, not Florida—I pulled to the side of the road to read Simmons' account of what and where my next stop would be. While thus occupied, a car pulled up beside me and the driver inquired if I was searching for the Trail. I replied in the affirmative. She and the other two adult passengers invited me to their home so they could acquaint me with the Trail sites in this and the Durham locale. I accepted, but stated I needed to think about where to find lodging for the night, realizing my choices were probably no better than the previous night. No problem, they chimed in; a telephone call to "the" Hillsboro motel would take care of that concern. And that was my introduction to the Vogt family.

There were Pat and Jack, their two grown daughters Chris and Debbie, and Debbie's boys Michael and Matthew. The conversations—there were several running concurrently—covered much of the family's history, the history of their fine circa 1910 house (which boasted more stained glass than many churches), their horses and breeding of same, and, of course, the Santa Fe Trail. As darkness settled over the countryside several hours later, I managed to extricate myself from this charming, garrulous family, but not before Jack had made arrangements for the tour we would take the next morning. As I departed, an act that took much effort on my part, Pat thrust a book into my hands which she and Chris jointly authored commemorating Durham's centennial, and Chris followed with another of their published creations, this one about the orphan trains which extended from 1854 to 1929 which relocated orphans from New York City to Kansas and other Midwestern states (Vogt, Martha Nelson, Chris Vogt, *Searching for Home*, 1986). As I cruised down the road toward Hillsboro, I was surrounded by a feeling of disbelief and euphoria as I pondered over the past several hours.

Durham, Kansas, a lively village boasting roughly a dozen more citizens than Tampa's one hundred thirteen, is quite proud of its Santa Fe Trail heritage. The night before in my motel room I had perused Pat and Chris' history of the town, discovering much more about the Trail than either Simmons or Gregory Franzwa had recorded. I also surmised from what I had observed about the Vogts that Jack had planned much more than my time would allow—I had an appointment with more Trail buffs that afternoon one hundred sixty-five miles west. The lesson that continually is brought home as I explore the Trail is that no matter how much time and flexibility is allowed, the former is always exhausted before all the latter has been provided for. This day was to be the same.

Near the appointed hour Jack pulled up beside my Cherokee and we headed down a gravel road for Cottonwood Crossing. By the time we had seen several fine ruts and markers it was time to head for our rendezvous with Dennis Youk, manager of the ranch upon which the dramatic "Durham Blowout" rests. This is arguably the most breathtaking set of ruts along the entire stretch of the Trail. Their spectacular appearance is due to severe erosion primarily from wind, thereby creating a gully, in places over twelve feet deep. As we tooled down the road Jack recognized an approaching auto, not Dennis but the rest of the Vogt family who had decided they could not pass up the excursion. From there we caravanned to where I would meet Dennis and the Durham Blowout.

Dennis did not disappoint me any more than had the many other gregarious and hospitable down-home Kansas folks I have been privileged to meet. In this I am perplexed by Heat-Moon who did not appear to encounter such with any frequency. What a loss for him and his readers. Dennis led us in his pickup to where we would enter the field. He left us there, but not without inviting me to his house to see an aerial photo of the Blowout.

With varying degrees of agility and awkwardness, each of us climbed the forbidding barbed wire fence in a huge pasture and headed toward the first set of ruts. Michael and Matthew raced ahead excitedly, calling out as they discovered yet another rut or evidences of wildlife. At first the ruts were standard swales, highlighted by their dark vegetation. As we mounted a slight rise, we looked down upon several natural tiny pools, and beyond we gained our first true sight of the Blowout. But it was not until some minutes later when we actually entered between its walls was its true awesomeness impressed upon me. Whow! I stooped to touch the very active soil that I imagined could change its contour almost at will, much like a sand dune. The shouting boys' voices pulled me back from the imagined sounds of insistent bullwhackers, protesting animals, creaking wagon wheels, and even an isolated child's laughter. Michael and Matthew were standing on the eroding rim some fifteen feet above me. And so our hike continued up this strange canyon and back. Although rock is scarce in this field, I did find a black gnarled stone that I took for poe-poe lava rock to add to my growing Santa Fe Trail rock collection. Rocks, long a source of intriguing wonder for me, help me connect with the Trail more vividly. As I hold each one, tracing its contours with fingers, it seems that the reality of Trail life is transferred from stone to my person, and I am there, walking beside a team of swaying oxen.

Back in my Cherokee we returned to Cottonwood Creek in search of the crossing. The steep bank precluded every logical spot until I discovered a long, yet steep overgrown cut-down which I decided was the crossing. It was easy to understand why this crossing posed such great problems, as reported time and again in various diaries. One of the less disastrous calamities (or was it?), reported by Lewis Garrard, was the loss of two boxes of claret from a wagon that overturned in attempting to obtain the crest of the steep bank.

This was also a region of cruel and violent blizzards where

both men and cattle gave their last full measures. In the January 28, 1842 edition of the *Rushville* [Indiana] *Whig,* it was reported that a local citizen headed for Santa Fe froze to death. "The storm they [the caravan] encountered was very violent, and the snow fell to the depth of two or three feet—it was much drifting in places, so that it was almost impossible to travel."[12]

Yet there were more joyful events at Cottonwood Crossing, and nothing can match David Kellogg's diary entry on September 26, 1858. "The comet," he wrote, "has been very brilliant for the last two evenings; it stretches clear across the Western sky. The great firebrand and the glittering stars make night seem enchantment...."[13] That would have been Donati's Comet, named for the Italian astronomer, Giovanni Battista Donati who discovered it in 1858.

All too soon it was time for me to move on, and again I was to feel the sadness of extending goodbyes to newfound friends. Pat presented me with a huge bouquet of native grasses she had picked at the Crossing, wishing such good luck for me as these had brought her. My last glance of them was through my camera viewfinder as they gathered around the Cottonwood Crossing DAR marker.

One more stop before barreling down to Offerle, my next rendezvous, was at the Youk farmhouse. There, Martha showed me the spectacular aerial photo of the Blowout. Had a Piper Cub been parked in a nearby pasture, I would not have been content until I was aloft viewing this incredible sight with my own eyes. Dennis came in for lunch, beaming over my reaction. He invited me to join them for a MacDonald's burger. My, how dining habits on the farm have changed.

Much to my dismay, I was forced to pass up sites on the Hillsboro-McPherson leg—yet more items to add to the lengthening list for the next trek.

Note: Taking another fast forward to 2009, we spent the night in Hillsboro. My previous stay in this college town (Tabor College, a Mennonite institution) was at a motel much pleasanter than this one. But, we survived. Early the next morning we headed for ruts in the Durham area which had recently been marked by Steve Schmidt and members of the SFTA Cottonwood Crossing chapter. Steve had designed a route marked by "Santa Fe Trail Crosses Here" standard road signs. Forty-seven—count them, forty-seven—signs have been erected. These were easy to follow, and no map was needed. However, upon approaching the primitive road, I was not sure I wanted to drive my somewhat clean car on the muddy road before me. Several days of heavy rains had created a quagmire. Nonetheless, I forged ahead, hoping conditions would improve, which they did. The route took us by the famous Durham Blowout, but even though I took every section line road around the ruts, they never were visible. I did not expect success, but did not abandon the thought. Although we did not see these famous ruts, there were others to excite us. This tour required almost two hours, but did not bring us any closer to Santa Fe, which was over six hundred miles away. Reluctantly, I headed my Jeep west.

Returning to the earlier (1991) tour, in Offerle I discovered that my tour guides included three generations of Trail buffs—Lynda Burghart, her father Jim Liebl, and her two-year-old son, Ben. It was my understanding that we would be viewing Dry Route sites recently rediscovered. The first stop was yet another pasture, this one occupied by timid cattle who ran from us even before we had slickly negotiated the barbed wire fences. Jim deftly separated two strands, and by crouching, we easily passed through. Western Kansas was in the grip of a severe drought, so swales and rut crowns, all devoid of vegetation, looked much the same. The next pasture, ruts, and cattle, well within sight of the Arkansas River, belonged to Paul Wetzel.

A bit of history about the Wet/Dry route is in order. The two traces ran roughly between Fort Larned and Fort Dodge, paralleling one another. Leading authorities have claimed, and this is verified by extant data, that the Wet Route hugs the river while the Dry crosses an arid stretch a few miles north. Logical, one would say. However,there is an ongoing debate among local Trail buffs about the designated names. Some say the Dry is actually the Wet, or the north route if one finds it easier to keep things straight with compass points. As for the Wet Route, it has also been called the Water Road, and it is south of the North Route. Just to confuse us even more, the Wet Route was always the preferred one during the dry season. I doubt if I will ever again be able to keep the two straight even if the argument is settled to the satisfaction of all.

Mule Head Hill, a landmark on the western horizon, was our next destination. On a broad summit of this modest rise in the middle of a plowed field stood another DAR marker. At the base it carried its own personally unique carving of a mule's head. Of the Trail guides and texts I use as references, I have not found mention of this site. Note: I have returned to this marker numerous times, but have never again been able to definitively identify the mule carving. Even the DAR notation is quite faint.

There were more ruts and markers to be visited, but once again the setting sun forced its will onto me. And once again I was reminded that a great deal of time is needed to follow the Trail today, perhaps as much as when it was the only road to Santa Fe. Before heading my Cherokee toward Dodge City, Jim invited me to his lovely home to see some of the artifacts he had found in the area over many years of walking the plains with eyes glued to the ground, including pottery shards, arrow points, bits of glass, and, of greatest interest, an arrow point embedded in a fragment of bison bone. Wife Velma had just taken freshly baked cookies from the oven, and with lemonade in one hand and the other free for cookies, I consumed my fair share— and more.

The night in Dodge City was uneventful. The waning light and late hour compelled me to pass up Santa Fe Park, which had eluded me on my last visit, and must wait for a later day.

A cold front had descended on western Kansas overnight, and I was greeted by a *bona fide* frost-dotted autumn the next morning. A few miles west of Dodge City just off highway U.S. 50 is a large stone monument commemorating Forts Mann and Atkinson and the Caches. No evidence of any of these famous sites remains today. Even the depressions in the ground, which were once large holes, have since been filled in. These were where two traders, James Baird and Samuel Chambers, cached their goods over a bitter winter while they journeyed to Taos to replace their livestock that had succumbed during an arctic blizzard. I am always saddened when confronted with accounts of the loss of even a single memento carrying the Trail's life-blood within it. Man and his creations on the one hand are most fragile, yet bear everlastingness on the other.

The nippy weather persisted as I walked a set of well-preserved ruts nine miles west of Dodge at the Boot Hill Museum, the west unit of a museum located on Dodge City's famous Front Street, a re-creation of the unruly, outlaw town infamous in the nineteenth century. Franzwa's Trail guide contains an excellent aerial photo of these ruts.[14]

This was definitely short grass prairie. The expansive view, punctuated by the ubiquitous grain elevators, seemed to contradict the fact that once this country was black as far as the eye could see with grazing buffalo. Man's intentional mission to destroy an entire species—over fifty million strong—in less than a decade, is a frightening indictment against "Yankee ingenuity" and "manifest destiny." The carnage is also the legacy of the Santa Fe Trail, although rarely acknowledged. Romance, valor, high drama, and danger—this is what we want to crowd our memories, but not genocide—of beasts and humans—greed, and selfishness. All haunt the Trail today, and like Morley's ghost, are shackled to the grizzly truth of deeds forged when the Trail was alive.

I had been following the Arkansas River all morning, that enigmatic waterway which brought forth the full range of reactions from those who encountered it. A mile wide and an inch deep by someone's calculations, it was riddled with sinkholes and quicksand. John W. Moore, a veteran wagonmaster, gave his account of an 1867 crossing. "We doubled the teams," he wrote, "making sixteen mules to each wagon, and sometimes put on the third team. Because of quicksand..., we had six drivers to each wagon to lash the mules and keep them moving. But even at that it took the entire day to make the crossing."[15]

Matt Field saw a much different Arkansas, and he sang its virtues in verse:

> The "Arkansaw" in the noon-day beam
> Is a beautiful and grassy stream.
> With its Buffalo herds on its banks of green,
> And its fairy-like Islands that lie between,
> Is a sight, in the sun or the moonlight sheen
> Lovely and beautiful to be seen.[16]

A footnote about Field's poetry is in order. Employing verse to record events was unique among Trail chroniclers except as an isolated line or two to punctuate a theme. However, Field very often chose poetry to express his emotions, and describe the drama that unfolded each day. For a full month during his first journey, from the mirage-creating Sand Hills along the Arkansas River to the intimidating Raton Pass, he "spoke" in "heroic couplets," Sunder's introductory words, p. xxiv. How fortunate we are to have this "romantic" narrative.

But the Arkansas River I saw beside Cimarron Crossing Park in Cimarron, KS, which marks the Middle Crossing—there were three primary crossings, and many others used on occasion when the river's quixotic nature demanded or allowed—presented neither picture. It was nothing more than a dry bed overgrown with dense vegetation that easily concealed whatever isolated pools may have managed to survive the present irrigation-driven culture. Quicksand in the U.S.? Somehow I always associated that dread natural devourer of material of all sorts with Africa, South America, and other genuinely "wild" regions of our planet. Yet, here it was in my own corner of the continent. Maybe no longer, but certainly an ever-present vexation for trailers.

The morning was quickly slipping away, and since I still faced 500 miles of driving that day, I was compelled to pass up several outstanding sites. When I originally charted my course for this trip, I had no intention of including any of western Kansas, but my willpower is so fragile when approaching any Trail site, and I usually find my Cherokee turning off the road, almost demonstrating a mind of its own. Now I must be resolute, however. Only a few more stops and then I simply must head for home. But first I could not bypass Charlie's Ruts, several miles west of Deerfield. Here the prairie is definitely giving way to desert. These swales, on property donated to Kearny County Historical Society by Paul Bentrup, are sprinkled with yucca, prickly pear cactus, and an assortment of other desert vegetation. Paul, a devout Trail addict and Santa Fe Trail Association founder, has marked the ruts with small flags on wire standards. Thank you, Paul, for the guidance.

At Lakin I could not resist stopping at the Kearny County museum for but a brief glimpse of the conestoga wagon on display.

Although the museum was closed (natch!), the door was open, and the friendly director allowed me to see it. As it would happen, she too was a Trail buff. This was my introduction to Pat Heath, and the beginning of a special friendship. We exchanged addresses and, with my promise to return the next spring and visit the museum when it was open, I headed south on Kansas Highway 25. I was now following the Cimarron Cutoff.

No more stops. Well, the pullout above Wagon Bed Spring hardly counts. Here was another fine Mormon Battalion marker, a Kansas historical marker denoting the Spring, and a monument commemorating Jedediah Smith, legendary mountain man and explorer who was killed by Comanches at some unknown site in this vicinity. Looking down from this lofty perch, the tree-lined bank clearly outlined the Cimarron River's course.

Continuing a southward direction, I tried to see the terrain as through the eyes of the original travelers, a frequent exercise I have adopted. On this treacherous leg of the Cutoff, what thoughts sprang to their minds as they viewed the chamisa and sage landscape that seemingly extended even beyond the distant horizon. In fact, William Napton hardly saw the country through which his train passed because they traveled at night to avoid the searing heat of the "jornada," Spanish for an arduous stretch of dry desert. Perhaps it was due to the darkness that he accidentally laid down in a bed of cactus to catch a brief rest.[17] Ouch!

There were no visible landmarks, at least no famous ones, so I tried to create them. Even the most modest change I tried to imagine as a sentinel pointing toward Santa Fe. Suddenly, in front of me a herd of a dozen pronghorn antelope appeared at the side of the road. I was elated to see these graceful little creatures, and in Kansas, at that. Yet, when Josiah Gregg made his first journey west in 1831 he noted that they were sometimes seen as far east as Council Grove—300 miles east of this spot.[18] This was the first time I recall seeing antelope in Kansas, although they are a common sight in New Mexico. I slowed and pressed my hand to the horn. Fortunately, they slowly turned away from the road momentarily, waiting for the coast to clear. The antelope's life may be a bit safer today than during the Trail era. They too were wantonly slaughtered, their natural curiosity often placing them unnecessarily in danger's path. However, high speeding autos can be as lethal as high-powered rifles. I silently thanked those lovely pronghorn for giving me another special glimpse inside the Santa Fe Trail fraternity.

Cruising through Boise City, Oklahoma, I sternly lectured myself to keep moving rather than take a detour to Flag Spring, Autograph Rock, McNees Crossing, Cold Spring, and all those other dramatic sites in the Oklahoma panhandle which were calling to me as clearly as those sirens of yore luring sailors onto cataclysmic rocks. Now if only the winter would pass quickly so that I could experience those prizes that to date had been just beyond my reach.

Approaching Clayton, New Mexico, while still in Oklahoma, the trail travelers gained their first glimpse of the mountains, or more accurately, a sort-of mountain. And so did I. Rabbit Ears (Mountain) rises up quite dramatically from an otherwise level plain. It was an unforgettable landmark that signaled to all that the plains were behind them and the mountains—and Santa Fe—in front. Each time I pass it, I too feel that the sight of a mountain signifies I am home. Considering that I have resided in the mountains for only eight of my many years, I never cease to be amazed at the strength of my bond with them.

On past Clayton I drove. Off to the north I spied Mt. Dora and Round Mound, and farther west, Point of Rocks and Wagon Mound. The landmarks that I have come to know so well over the past several years came quickly upon one another: fine ruts which parallel highway I-25; the road to Fort Union and Tiptonville; Watrous, Sapello stage station and the nearby stone corral; Las Vegas with its Trail wealth spread through the town and surrounding countryside. All the way into Santa Fe I scanned the terrain both left and right, vividly recalling what lay down the various roads and the history represented there.

I passed through Apache Canyon and made the final ten-mile run into Santa Fe, and the memories of these four days already commenced to pour over me. It would be some time before I would review in detail what I had seen, but first I must make a list of what I had *missed* for future reference. For the moment, I simply let the aura of Trail fever well up and consume me. Figuratively, I tipped my hat in respect to all the brave and foolhardy who were not content to live their lives east of Kansas Territory in relative safety and comfort, but instead, irresistibly embarked upon an adventure which launched them—and we who followed—into a brave new world.

Notes

1. Majors, Alexander. *Seventy Years on the Frontier.* Lincoln, Nebraska: University of Nebraska Press, 1989, p. 71.

2. Drumm, Stella (Ed.). *Down the Santa Fe Trail and Into Mexico.* Lincoln, Nebraska: University of Nebraska Press, 1982, p. 10.

3. Barbour, Barton H. (Ed.). *Reluctant Frontiersman: James Ross Larkin on the Santa Fe Trail, 1856–57.* Albuquerque, New Mexico: University of New Mexico, 1990, pgs. 71-72.

4. Davis, W.W.H. *El Gringo: New Mexico and Her People.* Lincoln, Nebraska: University of Nebraska Press, 1982, pgs. 21-22.

5. *Ibid.,* p. 24.

6. Drumm, *op. cit.,*p. 10.

7. *Ibid.,* p. 17.

8. Garrard, Lewis. *Wah-to-yah and the Taos Trail.* Norman, Oklahoma: University of Oklahoma Press, 1955, p. 15.

9. Russell, Marian. *Land of Enchantment: Memoirs of Marian Russell Along the Santa Fe Trail.* Albuquerque, New Mexico: University of New Mexico Press, 1981, p. 18.

10. Sunder, John E. (Ed.). *Matt Field on the Santa Fe Trail.* Norman, Oklahoma: University of Oklahoma Press, 1960, pgs. 79, 77.

11. Drumm, *op. cit.,* p. 22.

12. *Wagon Tracks*, 1989, 4(1), pg. 15.

13. David Kellogg's Diary, 1858. In Marc Simmons (Ed.) *On the Santa Fe Trail.* Lawrence, Kansas: University Press of Kansas, 1986, p. 55.

14. Franzwa, Gregory. *The Santa Fe Trail Revisited.* St. Louis, Missouri: The Patrice Press, 1989, p. 122.

15. Moore, John W. Trail Trip, 1867. In *Dawson Scrapbooks,* "Trails and Forts," *Wagon Tracks,* 1990, pgs. 4(2), 17.

16. Sunder, *op. cit.,*pgs. 28-29.

17. Napton, W.B. *Over the Santa Fe Trail in 1857.* Kansas City, Missouri: Franklin Hudson Publisher, 1905, pgs. 34, 36.

18. Gregg, Josiah. *The Commerce of the Prairies.* Milo Milton Quaife (Ed.). Lincoln, Nebraska: University of Nebraska Press, 1967, p. 42.

Minor Park ruts, Kansas City, Missouri.

Alexander Majors house, Kansas City, Missouri.

Madonna of the Trail sculpture, Council Grove, Kansas.

Diamond Spring, Kansas.

Lost Spring, Kansas.

Durham Blowout. Durham, Kansas.

4

Back to Council Grove

On April 24, 1992 I found myself back in Council Grove, this time with a friend, Janice Blevins, who was experiencing Kansas for the first time. It had taken us all day to drive the 260 miles from Tulsa, since we insisted on stopping at every historic or scenic site we came upon. None were Trail-related, of course, since our route was south of the famous road. However, the flavor of the Trail was in all we saw, particularly noticeable when we first beheld the bluestem tall grass prairie in northern Oklahoma.

A quotation by John C. Van Tramp poetically describes the prairies, while recognizing that their flavor can never be captured in words. He said:

> There is no describing [the prairies]. They are like the ocean in more than one particular but in none more than this: the utter impossibility of producing any just impression of them by description. They inspire feelings so unique, so distinct from anything else, so powerful, yet vague and indefinite, as to defy description, while they invite the attempt.[1]

Thus, by the time we drove into Council Grove, dusk had overtaken us. Our home for the next two days would be the Cottage House Hotel, one of twelve registered historic structures in this town of two thousand three hundred souls. We dined at Hays House, of course, which provides a fitting companion to the Cottage House. We were seated in the second floor tavern because, much to my surprise, the dining room was filled. Actually, without reservations, we were fortunate to have been seated at all. In such a tiny town, far from any metropolitan area of even modest size, in the month of April—the restaurant's reputation notwithstanding—I wondered from whence the diners hailed.

Although the Trail officially birthed it, this town beside the Neosho River had been the crossroads for many other travelers long before William Becknell first caught sight of the lush hardwood forests that bounded the river as far as the eye could see. But, it was the rich soil of the prairies and the indomitable spirit of those pioneers who set out to tame it that breathed life into that helpless infant and nurtured it to adultood. This spirit still thrives, as we were to discover very quickly.

The next morning we took continental breakfast in the hotel dining room, seated aound the large table which we shared with the other guests. Immediately, we were engagd in a lively conversation with a group fom Garden City. It was not surprising to learn that we had mutual friends from there—the small world syndrome again. Most of them were familiar with Council Grove's preeminent Trail status, but that was only incidental to their reason for visiting the town. I could only wonder if their interest would be piqued as they visited all of the local sites, Trail related and other.

Following breakfast I asked the hotel desk clerk if it would be possible to visit the Seth Hays house and the Last Chance store, both which were closed during my previous visit. She gave me two names to call. Although my first attempt failed, I eventually reached Helen Prater, owner of the Last Chance store, who graciously agreed to allow us to see the store later in the day. Noon arrived, but still no success gaining access to the Seth Hays house. Again, the obliging desk clerk came to our asistance with another name, Betty Dutton, who might be "nooning" at the Hays House. As we entered the restaurant the hostess called out a cheery greeting. Yes, she remembered me from my visit last October, and she had heard we were looking for Betty. No, Betty had not been in, but a telephone call brought her in five minutes. Seth's house is open only by advance appointment. and presumably, in Council Grove five minutes is advance enough.

Seth M. Hays was the first permanent white resident in the area, arriving in 1847. Among his illustrious ancestors were greatgrandfaher Daniel Boone and cousin Kit Carson. He built the first log cabin on the site of the present restaurant which bears his name. In 1867 he built the brick house in which we were now standing with Betty. It was a simple yet comfortable five room cottage, modest by today's standards, but when built was a mansion in a place where twenty years before only a massive unbroken prairie existed. Just two blocks off the Trail, the house never heard the clamorous sounds of Trail traffic, for by then the lowing of the patient oxen, the calls of the bullwhackers, and the crack of their whips had been replaced by the mournful wale of a train whistle.

Believing her job not yet completed, Betty suggested that we swing by the Morris County Museum located at the site of the Post Office Oak. The native limestone building, originally built as a brewery and home in 1864 by a German immigrant, stands guard over the remains of a huge oak tree with a stone cache at its base. Travelers used this tree as a mail box to leave messages for those who followed behind them or to be forwarded by others headed in the opposite direction. Most interesting in the museum's collection of nineteenth century "everything" was the cellar of the stucture itself, which was large enough to receive a team and wagon through its large double doors. Because the ground sloped at the end of the building where the doors were located, these were at ground level, not below ground. Could this have been the first bi-level house west of the Mississippi?

As we bade Betty goodbye, thanking her profusely for her warmth of spirit and generosity of time, I again was reminded that Kansans' gregariousness is unmatched. We had to hurry if we wanted to see the ruts on the west side of town before meeting Helen at the Last Chance store. As expected, it was necessay to drive down a gravel road to find them. After taking one wrong turn and then backtracking, I finally found the right road where a sign marked the Trail's crossing. A gentle rise in a northeast pasture easily revealed ruts descending to a thicket of trees and shrubs on the southeast side. These were the first ruts Janice had ever seen. I cannot say she was awed—this was a modest track— but, she was amazed that they had survived for well over a century. We had to be content with viewing them from behind fences, but I am confident that had we gone to the nearby farmhouse, we would have been granted permission to walk the Trail by the current owner. Such is the pride and interest Kansans have in the Santa Fe Trail.

Rushing back to town, we pulled to the curb beside the Last Chance store just as Helen alighted from her car at her house, which is next door. Leading us through the rickety door whose rusty hinges, from all appearance, would soon disintegrate, she told us the colorful history of the building.

Built in 1857 of native sandstone by Thomas C. Hill, it supplied Santa Fe-bound caravans for but a short four years. Later, it would serve as a post office, government trading post, and private residence. Presently, it houses the overflow from Helen's antique shop next to the Cottage House Hotel. Once a year, during Wah-Shun-Gah Days, the town festival celebrating the famous Kaw Indian chief of the same name, it relives its glory days. However, scanning the shelves which displayed antiques of varying quality and use, I doubt that Trail travelers could have found any utilitarian purposes for their contents. Helen expressed deep concern about the rapidly deteriorating roof, windows, doors, and, in fact, the entire structure. She had unsuccessfully applied for a grant from the Kansas Heritage Trust Fund to restore the small store. Disappointed but not daunted, she plannd to pursue other funding sources. The loss of this prime Trail site would be calamitous. Hopefully, someone will come foreward with the bucks to prevent such.

Desiring to see the magnificent Seth Hays barn before sunset, I asked Helen for directions. Although the barn is clearly visible from U.S. 50 east of town, finding the right dirt road leading to it is not that simple. Because I had failed to find it on my last Council Grove visit, I pumped Helen with more questions than was actually necessary, as it turned out. We drove out the highway and located the proper road with no difficulty. The huge structure looming in the distance grew to gigantic proportions by the time we arrived at its base. 'Twas hard to imagine how one could avoid it. (Several months later Helen wrote, apologizing that she had not personally guided us to the barn, worryng all the while that we may have been forced to move on without reaching our goal. She was pleased when I reported that her directions were sound, and I was keen enough to follow them.)

The 76x40x40 foot barn was built by Hays in 1871, over four years after the railroad blazed a new trail some forty miles north, thereby ostensibly dissolving the long-standing marriage between Council Grove and the Santa Fe Trail. This fact notwihstanding, I believe the barn, too, is wedded to the Trail, thus the reason I chose to visit it. The Heart of the Flint Hills chapter of the Santa Fe Trail Asociation is engaged in a mammoth restoration project of the barn. And none too soon. Walls were listng dangerouly, stones had become dislodged and had fallen to the ground, and wood throughout had rotted. Yet, the majesty of the structure shone through the debris. We could only hope that the funds to restore the barn will be forthcoming. How often I have remarked thusly about the numerous structures along the Trail that need tender loving care—and *money*.

The next moning we left town, but the aura remained with us for some time—and still does. Kansas is noted for other attractions than the Santa Fe Trail, and I wanted Janice to experience some of these as well. Lindsborg, the unofficial Swedish capital of the U.S., was a logical choice. We toured shop after shop overflowing with colorful Swedish arts and crafts, and liberally dined on tasty smorgasbord treats. Then on we drove to Salina with its skyscraper grain elevators closing in the town on all sides.

Two days later we were following the Trail again—Ralph's Ruts, Pawnee Rock, Fort Larned, and aromatic Dodge City. Janice's sensitive nose demanded that our hotel be upwind, and I heartily concurred. In Dodge City we spent more time with Wyatt Earp than with William Becknell's descendents, but by the time we exited the state at Elkhart, Janice had gained some sense of Kansas' substantial contribution to the Trail and other cultural and physical offerings to our national heritage.

Note: On January 2, 1994 Helen Prater died quite unexpectedly. Before her death, a new roof had been installed on the Last Chance store. Ironically, it was made possible by damage from a violent storm, and replacement was covered by insurance. Connie Essington, the store's new owner, is perpetuating Helen's loving stewardship. Replastering is now underway.

Like so many Trail sites, I have been privileged to visit Council Grove on numerous occasions, and each time I discover more sites which contribute to the town's uniqueness, and more memories to accumulate. In 1997 an attractive riverwalk was consructed, along which were placed interpretive markers telling the story of the river crossing and the thick hardwood forest that lined its banks. One could walk from downtown up to the Kaw Mission, and in the process learn why Council Grove was a true luminary of the Trail.

Hermit's Cave, while famous in the Grove, also holds a New Mexico significance. The rock cave is perched on the edge of a hill above the west side of town. It was occupied for a time by an Italian, Matteo Boccalini. Upon further research, I found at least four sources, including Simmons and the Council Grove public relations brochure, which claim the hermit's name to be Giovanni Maria Augustini, although even they cannot agree on whether it is Italian or Spanish, the Spanish version being Juan Maria de Agostini. At least they agree on "Maria." He took holy orders in his homeland, but was forced to relinquish his position when rumors of a sexual scandal surfaced. He emigrated to the U.S., and eventually appeared in the Grove. For five months he lived in solitude, rarely communing with the few people in the area, then departed with a westbound wagon train, reputedly walking all the way to Santa Fe.[2] In northern New Mexico he found another cave in a mountain north of Las Vegas, Hermit's Peak, which was subsequently named for him. Gazing down amid the tree foliage onto Council Grove from Hermit's Cave, it certainly is a tranquil spot, and a perfect home for a contemplative.

Council Grove received its name from a grove of deciduous trees a mile wide beside the Neosho River under which a treaty was executed between the Osage Indians and the U.S. through its "representative" George Sibley who was conducting a government survey of the Trail in 1825. The trees were highly prized for Trail wagon repairs and spare parts. The oldest at this time, a Burr oak, has a sprout date (date the young tree first appeared) of 1694. The town is so proud of these ancient trees that they have been marked and identified on the self-guided auto historic tour.

A magnificent structure not to be overlooked is Seth Hays' stone barn just over a mile east of town, which I discovered during my 1992 visit. It was not until the 1999 SFTA Symposium hosted by Council Grove that I was able to get a close-up view of this imposing building. The Sunday morning session, which began with a scrumptious ranch breakfast (hay bale seating provided), was held at the barn, which was undergoing badly needed restoration. Among the presenters was Nancy Kassebaum Baker, retired U.S. senator from Kansas. The barn is on the National Register of Historic Places.

Note: On yet another occasion, that being the 2009 trek to the SFTA Symposium in Arrow Rock, Missouri, I was again back in Council Grove, again with my buddy, Faye Gaines. This time we took a side trip nineteen miles south to Cottonwood Falls, where the famous Chase County courthouse is located. This magnificent structure with its blazing red metal roof is the oldest courthouse in the U.S. still functioning as intended. The U.S. is noted for its architecturally outstanding courthouses, but in my view, none surpasses this gleaming fire engine-red-roofed edifice.

As I write, other sites in the larger Council Grove vicinity keep tumbling over one another in my mind, although what year I visited them I do not recall. Six-mile Creek crossing and stage station immediately come to mind. It was the custom to name the creeks in this area based on their distance from Diamond Spring, hence the Spring is six miles east of this creek. I had made a prior appointment with the property owner, Bonnie Sill, to visit, and after navigating from one gravelly section line road to another, successfully reached her farm. She guided me to the few remaining foundation stones of the stage buildings, a corral, and a well, all which were set in a shady grove. Faint ruts led down a slope to a primitive bridge crossing the now dry creek and up a grade into a fallow gold-weeded native pasture which was sprinkled with slender violet gayfeather blossoms. Bonnie exuded the typical hospitality I have found along the Trail. There was evidence in her house that she had dropped several tasks when I arrived, yet she gave the impression that she had all the time in the world to give me the complete tour and history. From the NPS "Santa Fe Trail Management and use Plan" I learned that the stage station opened about 1863, and closed in 1866 or 1867 when the stage line moved north to Junction City, Kansas. One constant in the U.S. is that roads move and with them go convenience, businesses, and often entire towns.

On yet another trek, whether before or after visiting Six-Mile Creek crossing and stage station I do not recall, my immediate goal was to find Ed Miller's grave on the "outskirts" of Canton, Kansas, a very, very small village ten miles east of McPherson. Ed's grave is located in the private Jones cemetery on a gravel road several miles north of U.S. 56. Ed's is a sad story. He was killed in an Indian attack as he was rushing to inform a homesteader family that their daughter was ill and wanted her mother to visit. It was a story that was repeated up and down the Trail. Of course, we do not know similar episodes that occurred among Native American nations. It was fitting that I should pay my respects to this brave young man. What is unique about the site is that a DAR marker is placed immediately next to Ed's headstone in no particular order. My next destination was Running Turkey campground, but trying to follow Gregory Franzwa's confusing written directions in his guidebook, *The Santa Fe Trail Revisited,* was an exercise in frustration, requiring frequent stops to read where I was next to go. All this could have been avoided had a detailed map been included, as is the style he and other authors have employed elsewhere in self-guided tour books

McPherson was but a few miles farther down the road. Although I had been there before, there were sites in this Trail-rich region that had escaped me. Thus, in 2002 when the SFTA Board of Directors meeting was being held in Lexington, Missouri, McPherson lay directly on the route from Santa Fe. As so often before, Faye Gaines and I joined forces for the trip. A local authority was needed to guide us, and the perfect person was Britt Colle who has been a strong force in the SFTA Quivira chapter, and with wife Linda is arguably the leading Trail authority in the area. Britt met us on the west edge of town, and we immediately headed for the most incredible series of ruts I have ever seen. These are in Joe Swanson's pasture on the east side of the Little Arkansas River. Eight or nine—yes, eight or nine—sets prominently show the Trail's descent down to the river. Faye and I could only repeatedly "ooh" and "aah." I took numerous photos, and in many views Faye and Britt were visible only from the waist up. I could only imagine the stupendous view from aloft.

Across the river, which we could only access by going a few miles around to the south, we came to the famous Marker Cottonwood, a huge tree which marks the river crossings. Walking along the rim of the steep bank, which was reported by Major Bennett Riley in 1829 to be fifteen feet high,[3] we tried to determine the precise cut bank down to the water, but even Britt, all his knowledge notwithstanding, was not sure. Everywhere we looked, it was obvious it would have been a hard climb both up and down. Yet it made no difference, for we were savoring the wildness of our surroundings.

Camp Grierson was our next stop. It is on the Little Arkansas River, a short distance south of the area we had just explored. Over the years the earth around the camp has preserved many of the configurations that help identify the site, specifically military trenches and breastworks. Also still visible are burial pits of over a dozen soldiers whose remains were moved to Fort Leavenworth in the late nineteenth century. This is a well-preserved site, and despite its brief tenure between 1865 and 1867, it deserves official status by either state or federal government agencies.

Britt led us to other sites as well as five DAR markers in the McPherson vicinity until the fading light forced us to call it quits for the day. But first, Linda and their daughter joined us for a welcome dinner at Applebees. Food at a franchise restaurant *can* be good as demonstrated by this one in McPherson. I ordered a shrimp Caesar salad, their most special specialty, in my view.

I think it can safely be said that this is the end of eastern Kansas, and that the next significant sites—and there are many, beginning in Lyons—will be covered elsewhere.

Notes

1. Van Tramp, John C. *Prairie and Rocky Mountain Adventures, 1858.* In William Least Heat-Moon, *PrairyErth.* Boston, Massachusetts: Houghton Mifflin, 1991, p. 21.

2. Brigham, Lalla Maloy. *The Story of Council Grove on the Santa Fe Trail.* Council Grove, Kansas: Morris County Historical Society, 1921, pgs. 128-31.

3. Colle, Britt and Linda. Trail Booklet, Santa Fe Trail Association Symposium, 2005, p. 15.

Last Chance Store, Council Grove, Kansas.

Seth Hays barn, Council Grove, Kansas.

Swanson's ruts, Little Arkansas River, Kansas.

Marker Cottonwood tree, Little Arkansas River, Kansas.

5

Picking Up Loose Threads

Although over the years I had clocked many miles in western Kansas and the Oklahoma panhandle traveling to visit family and friends in western Kansas, much of the Cimarron Cutoff Trail route had been passed over at sixty miles per hour as though I did not know of its existence. That was to change in June 1993 when I set out for the express purpose of touring that dry, unforgiving stretch of the Trail in southwest Kansas that was devoid of water for a seemingly endless sixty miles. Also included in the tour would be the section of the Mountain Route between Lakin, Kansas and Bent's Old Fort.

Planning my itinerary was tricky, consuming more hours than I am willing to admit. I would travel the Cimarron sector from west to east, whereas the Simmons and Franzwa guides lead the traveler in the opposite direction. I wrote each site on paper as presented in Simmons guide, starting at the bottom of the page. By the time I reached the top margin, my itinerary was organized as I would be traveling—from west to east.

I picked up the Trail a Clayton, New Mexico and headed west eighteen miles to the Rabbit Ears Campground. As I drove up to the neat white stucco ranch house with bright red roof and trim, I wondered what success I would have at this, my first stop. Although it appeared someone was on the premises, no one responded to my knock. I was not even met by the ever present ranch dogs. Sadly, I drove away wondering if this was an omen of things to come over the next five days.

My next stop was at a marvelous stretch of ruts in the Kiowa National Grassland. To reach the site required driving five miles on a New Mexico gravel road, the prospect which did not excite me, considering the state's reputation for often leaving maintenance of these back roads in God's hands. Much to my delight, I was proven wrong, and tooling along at fifty miles per hour was both possible and not a gut-wrenching experience.

At the site I was greatly rewarded with a fine interpretive plaque and a *bon fide* gate leading to a field that held the much eroded ruts. The eastern stretch was a wide swale presenting a prime example of contrast in vegetation, the hallmark of a wagon rut. The swale was a blanket of spring green while on both sides only clumps of desert grasses and cacti managed to exist. No animal life—wild or domestic—was in sight, but the idyllic song of the meadowlark was all about me. I definitely was in the prairies, and I longed for my former Kansas home, where each day all summer long I was greeted by the music of that happy bird. Wildlife biologist, Douglas H. Chadwick, wrote in a 1993 issue of *National Geographic,* "the meadow lark sings a song that is a distillation of daybreak—a pure, yellow burst, a breastful of glory-coming-over-the-rim-of-the-earth notes."[1] God knew what he (she) was about when giving the aviary symbol of the prairies to the most musical of all birds.

The story of events at the crossing of the North Canadian River in 1828 which gave McNees Crossing, my next stop, its name has been memorialized by almost every traveler of the day who possessed a pen or pencil. Two hapless young men—Daniel Munro and a McNees, whose first name has been lost over time, notwithstanding all those aforementioned writing implements—were ambushed at the crossing. Munro promptly died and McNees soon after beside the Cimarron River. (A few years after my visit, McNees' given name, Robert, was discovered.) Their deaths set off retaliation by traders first, then by Indians, all which reached such a fever pitch that military escorts were called into action the following year for all caravans traveling the Cutoff. Of course, the day I visited the famous site no such danger lurked about. I was quite alone as I stood at the summit of the wagon-blazed ramp which led down to the river. I gasped at a huge gash in the earth on what I supposed was the opposite bank of the river. Ruts such as these I did not know existed. Well, they don't. I was viewing the river as it rounded a bend which was concealed by steep banks. It is safe to say that no one will call on me to confirm or reject any suspected ruts.

Although I have lived much of my adult life in the western half of the U.S., I continue to be amazed at what are officially classified as rivers in the southwest. I grew up beside the mighty Ohio River. Now, that is a "real" river, not like the sand and rock canyon before me containing but a few stagnant-appearing pools. Yet, I knew that even a benign course such as this could turn into a vicious monster, given the right meteorological conditions, destroying all in its path.

Much of the sandstone which produced the solid riverbed over which the caravans safely traveled without fear of encountering quicksand, a danger at many crossings, was a rich gold color—not the luxurious mineral, per se, however. That color was missing in my collection of Santa Fe Trail rocks, so I searched for the perfect example from this historic site. With the help of a company of horned larks who called this beach "home," I found the beautiful specimen.

Now I crossed into the Oklahoma panhandle, following ruts much of the way. Gentle swales and intense colored vegetation revealed them on the otherwise undistinguishable landscape. I was now in an area rich in Trail sites, most which I probably would not be permitted to visit. Yet, I would try. As I pulled into Shirley and Dave Hutchison's, active SFTA members, drive, I was greeted by four noisily excited dogs—the first I had seen all day. Shirley and her two children came out to calm us all. Camp Nichols, the most famous site in this locale, was not available for viewing, she said. We chatted about the Trail in general, and she pointed out a fine set of ruts I had missed several miles west. The local historical society was meeting that evening in Boise City, to which she invited me. I bade dogs and all goodbye and retraced my steps to the missed ruts, which were outstanding, as Shirley promised.

The day was quickly passing and I still had much to see. It was easy to floorboard the accelerator on the almost empty secondary roads, but as I passed a car stopped by a highway patrolman, I realized the folly of such. Autograph Rock and Cold Springs were my destination. Autograph Rock was the first site on private property to be certified by the NPS on the Santa Fe National Historic Trail. Shortly before pulling into the ranchyard, which is located ten miles down a back road, the emergency light flicked on above the gas gauge. Barring an unexpected event, I could make it to Boise City, but no farther. Carol Sharp, who with her husband Dan own the Rock and Springs, came out with but one small dog to welcome me. We chatted a few minutes, and again I was invited to the historical society meeting.

Autograph Rock is situated in a particularly tranquil setting. A lovely meadow separates the bluff on which are carved hundreds of names of trailers who passed this way and Cold Springs. I am continually impressed when visiting such spots as, for example, this Rock, El Morro in western New Mexico, and Register Cliff near Guernsey, Wyoming on the Oregon Trail by the artistry of many of the people who unknowingly memorialized their presence by carving their names upon the sheer face of whatever geological formation was at hand. Some engravings are not too different from those found on cemetery gravestones, so professional in appearance they are.

What patience and time were demanded of the Autograph Rock calligraphers, which I find difficult could be summoned up in the midst of the arduous and dangerous life that was the Trail. Yet, it reinforces mankind's need for artistic expression in the search for a more complete and satisfying life. His search is never more urgent than when life is seemingly at its most perilous. Then, man must dig down within his soul, and when he does he encounters the arts. I was awakened rudely from my contemplation by the incessant humming of mosquitos swarming about my head, regularly landing on the abundance of bare skin available to them. This intrusion prompted me to speed up my tour.

Note: I have frequently been drawn back to Autograph Rock, but invariably a problem occurs which denies me access to one or more of the Trail sites on the ranch. Once, Carol took her valuable time to drive me to a significant rise on their range from which an excellent view of distinct ruts were visible. As I clicked my camera shutter, that all too familiar whirring sound reached my ears, indicating the last frame in the roll of film. And where was a new roll? In my car back at Sharp's house.

Several years later I was again afforded the opportunity to *attempt* to visit the Rock and nearby Cold Spring, the latter which is on Dan's parents property. Faye Gaines and I were returning from an SFTA event, and perhaps her presence is attributable to our success. Carol escorted us to the senior (Buck) Sharp's residence. This hospitable and open couple emulated so many other Trail protectors I have met over the years. We walked to the spring house, but apparently the spigot had been turned off, for no water issued forth. Near the Spring is a long rock ledge on which more names have been scratched—Inscription Rock. This ledge is set in a cool woods, which would have provided welcome relief following the hot and treacherous trek across the Cimarron "jornada."

Yet another important site in the vicinity which took much effort to visit is Camp Nichols, approximately ten miles west of Autograph Rock. The ruins are not open to the public except on special occasions, such which occurred in 1997 during SFTA's biennial symposium. The Camp was built in 1865, but occupied for only a few months. In spite of such a short tenure, it hosted two famous people: Camp commander Colonel Kit Carson and our own Marion Russell. Marion first met Kit while she was a young student at the Loretto Academy in Santa Fe. Their friendship was strong—he called her "little Maid Marion." I never tire of reading Marion's beautiful memoirs, and the following passage, which is set in the dugout which were she and husband Richard's quarters at the Camp, generates powerful emotions—even tears—to well up.

One morning the Colonel came leading his big black horse.... "Little Maid Marian," he said, "I have come to say Good-bye." His last words to me as he rode away were, "Now remember the Injuns will git ye if you don't watch out." I watched him as he rode away.... The black horse mingled with mirage on the horizon and thus it was that Kit Carson rode out of my life forever.[2]

Now to return to my earlier travelogue.

Regrettably, I did not go to the historical society meeting that evening because little of the evening remained when I finally settled into the last motel room in town and had lustily devoured a sizable pizza which I was prepared to stack against any five star gourmet fare placed before me. Such was my hunger.

Leaving town the next morning, I passed the first of two NPS auto tour signs. These eventually will be posted along the Trail's full length. I believe Lady Bird Johnson would approve of this "beautification" of the prairies. My next stop that morning was the Cimarron National Grassland ranger station at Elkhart, Kansas. There I met District Ranger Joe Hartman and his office associate, Dorothy. Again I was reminded of the hospitality of those I have met along the Trail. Joe updated me on the work being done at the Point of Rocks-Middle Spring complex to create a recreational area. The plan has been criticized in some quarters for its supposed compromise of Trail integrity.

Before I set out for the site to check for myself, I stopped at the Morton County Museum. The museum should have been open, but a "closed" sign hung in the window. "Here we go again," I moaned. Seeing that the door was open, I ignored the sign and entered the building, where I was welcomed heartily by a docent. This is yet another fine museum, capturing a healthy slice of the history of the area. Their pride and joy was a furnished replica of a dugout dwelling, but it was a collection of early radios that caught my attention. Among them were a small white tabletop RCA, the model I recall from my childhood home, and, of course, the familiar Philco.

As I drove into the section of the Cimarron National Grassland that borders its namesake river, the first noticeable change from my previous visit three years earlier was the limestone posts placed strategically along the Trail. Next, the deeply rutted road to Middle Spring had been graded and the waist-high weeds mowed. But, most obvious were the picnic tables, toilets, walking trail, and bridge across the pool. One could definitely argue that these accoutrements bore no relationship to the condition that existed when the area was a viable Trail site. Yet, this time I could approach the spring without fear of encountering a local resident slithering in the concealing grass. The last time I did not catch even a glimpse of water. I surmised that the heavy traffic of many caravans beat down the grass to a condition not too dissimilar from what mowers were now required to achieve. I did not object to that. As for the present man-made structures, well, I had no difficulty either mentally or visually blocking them from view as I walked the footpath around the large pool of water. The four photos

I took, all from different angles, confirm that. The peaceful view that spread before me as I ate lunch at a picnic table was not spoiled for me knowing that few Trail travelers, save Susan Magoffin, experienced the luxury of a dining table.

However, I was more disturbed by the sight before me as I wound up the road to the top of Point of Rocks. Signposts were visible all along the mesa top. All the instructions which must be posted in a human use area managed by a federal agency detracted from the otherwise clean line of the site and was much different from the view travelers experienced. The interpretive sign, which formerly sat distractingly atop the mesa, had been moved to the ledge just below the summit. That was a good move, in my judgment. My evaluation of the before and after at these significant sites is mixed.

Joe had mentioned a particularly fine set of ruts along the Cimarron River corridor a few miles east of Middle Spring. They crossed the dirt road that parallels this entire stretch and wound up a gentle rise to a stock corral. He was right. The eroded ruts were clearly visible. I drove up a narrow lane to the corral for a better view, slowly picking my way through a large herd of cattle. They all passively stared at me with those huge brown eyes, as cattle are wont to do. All except one chocolate brown bovine who protested loud and long over the invasion of her domain by me and my Cherokee.

Since leaving Middle Spring the prickly pear cacti had increased significantly in number and size, as Joe warned. The cattle and I were surrounded by a forest of short vertical pads bearing treacherously sharp barbs. How difficult it must have been for both man and beast to successfully navigate through this painful carpet. But, today the hazards were minimized, at least in my eyes, by the thousands of pale yellow blossoms gracing the plants. Most assuredly, the ideal time to visit this mini kingdom of cacti is June.

Next stop was Wagon Bed Spring, otherwise known as Lower Cimarron Spring. Here I could witness the restoration efforts of local Trail enthusiasts. A new wagon box had been buried in the now dry spring, and ruts have been identified by handsome posts.

How did Wagon Bed Spring get such a fanciful name, you ask? We may never know the truth, but at this time, at least four different groups of travelers have been credited with sinking the first wagon bed in the spring as a means of clarifying the water. Colorful mythology, maybe, but the spring hardly needed such to place it firmly in the annals of history, for the drama of battle around it, the agony of thirst in search of it, and the panic and grizzly death when it was not located sets this stretch of the Trail apart from all others in a distinctive manner.

Eight miles north of Wagon Bed Spring I reached the town of Ulysses and yet another museum. With but a half hour before closing, I had only enough time to skim over the Trail exhibit and a model train display, the latter which was still being constructed. The builder flipped the switch, and I watched in fascination as an Atchison, Topeka, and Santa Fe freight train wended its way through a miniature replicated section of Ulysses, complete with authentic scale model grain elevators, the originals which I had passed coming into town. How long had he been at this project, I asked him. A long time was his ambiguous reply. When did he expect to finish? He didn't know.

On to Lakin and the now extinct Chouteau's Island, formerly located in the now almost extinct Arkansas River. The closest viewing spot is from Indian Mound, which boasts another DAR marker. However, even a good pair of binoculars did not reveal even a hint of what could be construed as an island. More impressive to me was the unending expanse of open prairie, broken but occasionally by a barn or windmill. Even the ubiquitous grain elevator was missing.

The next morning I headed for the Kearny County Museum. My trip had been specifically planned so I could be in Lakin on a Thursday, one of the three days in the week the museum is open. Much to my horror, a sign on the door informed me of the new hours—afternoons only. An additional four hours in Lakin waiting for the doors to open was not part of my plan. Dare I hope for better luck next time?

Sadly, I drove away toward Colorado. In Holly, Colorado, four miles west of the Kansas border, famous for its namesake sugar company (or is it the reverse?), I headed for a reputedly Trail-era limestone barn. Having a penchant for old barns, whether it be a stately stone edifice or a humble "little red barn on a farm down in Indiana," I cannot pass by without stopping for a closer look. This one fit the former category. Two arched doors and a similarly designed loft opening gave the structure an artistic appearance not often seen on the prairies. The northeast corner had been extended beyond its basic rectangular shape, probably to accommodate several animal stalls, thus adding to its already pleasing style and massiveness. Small square openings along the sides were meant as defensive rifle slits in the event of hostile attack, so locals told Simmons. Waist-high weeds in front and fencing on the other sides prevented close-up examination, but nothing could still my imagination from conjuring up a romantic tale about this mighty building, which began with the hauling of the limestone from many miles distant over a rugged and dangerous trail.

Moving on to the Holly cemetery where fine ruts are to be seen, I was faced with a barbed wire fence separating me from them. By crawling on my stomach and keeping my head and rear down, I successfully eluded those wicked barbs. Here again were ruts easily identified by healthy, green vegetation. Fortunately, crawling back out was equally trouble free.

As I pulled into the driveway of Big Timbers Museum in Lamar, Colorado, the quietude told me that once again I had struck out. Just when would my luck change, I lamented. Lamar is home to one of the four Madonna of the Trail statues. It is located at a busy intersection on highway U.S. 50. I took a photo of it—with a Hardee's fast food sign in the background

Next stop was the ruins of Bent's New Fort. Simmons' map easily guided me down several section line roads. Seeking permission to enter the pasture where the ruins are located, I drove to the nearest house, surmising it to be the residence of the owners. There was no response to my repeated knocks, and fortunately, no over-protective dogs. To reach the ruins, again it was under a fence I had to a crawl.

The story behind why a second fort was built is one of the few dramatic tales which does not deal with death, although destruction is definitely central to its *raison d'etre*. In August of 1849 William Bent, for some unexplainable reason, moved all occupants and possessions from the original fort, which was thirty miles upriver from this spot. He then put a torch to the structure. Because he never publicly explained his actions, we are left to wonder. David Lavender[3] suggests that he was despondent over the premature deaths of his three brothers, and rather than sell to the U.S. Army or abandon it to the Indians, he chose to destroy it. Another speculation is that he had always wanted the fort to be built in these Big Timbers, but his partners, brother Charles and Ceran St. Vrain, thought otherwise. Now with Charles dead and Ceran out of the business, he was free to exert his will. Whether this or any of the other numerous theories put forth is the actual case may never be known. Perhaps it is irrelevant, except to those who desire to understand the mind and soul of William Bent.

The fort was located on a gentle rise with a commanding view of the Arkansas River and the prairies that stretched in all directions. This was the Big Timbers section of the river that so many travelers wrote about. The giant cottonwood trees are long gone—since 1863, by historian Stanley Vestal's[4] reckoning—harvested to provide fuel and wagon parts. The outline of the fort was clearly discernible, although now reduced to earthen mounds with stones strewn upon them.

Over the years of Trail-trekking I have learned from the veterans to constantly scan the ground for artifacts. Tin cans and glass fragments are common at Trail sites, but few date from that period. Not being able to accurately identify a soldered can—the sealing process used then—I am reduced to examining each rusty can, only to place it back on the ground wondering what I have found. One flattened can among those ruins did attract my attention, however. It was the shape for sardines or oysters, common foodstuffs transported on the Trail. This artifact I kept, and discovered later that it was from the Trail era, identifiable by several ribbons of solder laid down at the joints. Admittedly, I should not have moved it from the ruins, and am prepared to return it when the Fort is officially preserved as a Santa Fe Trail site.

About a mile due west is the site of the first Fort Lyon,[5] but I had to drive several section line roads to come within two hundred yards of the ruins. The fenced, cultivated field which held them was not very inviting with its "No Trespassing" signs menacingly posted, thus I elected not to crawl under the fence this time. I had to be content with viewing the supposedly extensive ruins through binoculars. It was apparent that something besides freshly plowed soil was in that field, but only a vivid imagination could claim these to be the crumbling foundations of Fort Lyon.

Several miles farther down yet another dirt road I located another DAR marker, this one in the midst of fine ruts. A few hundred yards toward the south was the Arkansas River again. At this spot I was happy to see that some "big timbers" actually existed. Could it be possible that at some time in the not too distant future this section of the river will once again lay legitimate claim to its colorful title?

Returning to U.S. 50 I noticed Hud's Campground sign. Simmons mentions it in the directions to aforementioned DAR marker. I walked up to a man who was mowing the grass and asked if I could photograph the office building because this was a Trail site. He had not heard of his property's fame, but then he had owned it only about seven years. I said there might be artifacts on the premises. As I returned to my car I was prompted for some unknown reason to read that sentence in the guidebook. Much to my embarrassment, no reference is made to the campground as a Trail era site. Simmons mentions it simply as a reference point for locating the previous DAR marker. Often I think of that gentleman with his metal detector, scanning the grounds in vain day after day. I do owe him an apology.

Ever so slowly I was working my way to Bent's Old Fort, the point where I would pick up the section of the Trail I previously had explored. The picnic ground at John Martin Reservoir was a fine location for a late lunch. Although most of the old Trail in this vicinity is now under water, a section of ruts overlooking the lake has been preserved. At such times I am made painfully aware of the many conflicting and questionable priorities humans establish. Could not another less intrusive location for the reservoir been selected? Is flood control even needed? No doubt hydrology specialists would think me most naïve. Why must nature, and in this case, history, always fall victim to man's lust for "progress?" A short distance below the reservoir dam I located Red Shin's Standing Ground, a Trail landmark which, remarkably, has been saved from a watery grave. There is a story behind the mushroom-shaped rock, of course. Red Shin and another Cheyenne quarreled over a woman. When the other called in his relatives for assistance, Red Shin scooped up all the weapons he could carry, scampered up the odd shaped rock, and successfully drove them from the field of battle. Instantly, the rock acquired a name, and it was not "Point of Rocks."

My next stop was new Fort Lyon (there certainly was a lot of moving about in those days), now a Veterans Administration Hospital. While most of the impressive college campus style buildings post-date the period when it was a military installation, some original officers quarters, though much remodeled, and two large limestone warehouse structures are still standing. With the parade ground now carpeted with a well manicured lawn overarched by a dense grove of huge (cottonwood?) trees, it is difficult to imagine that once this complex was barren of most vegetation, totally open to the blue sky and a brilliant sun.

The house where Kit Carson died in 1868 has been converted into a chapel. With its steep pitched roof, steeple, and asphalt parking lot at the door, it little resembles its original state, that being the modest residence of the post surgeon. It was just as well the door was locked and I could not see the even more startling changes that the interior no doubt has undergone. Oh well, at least it is still standing.

Note: Several decades later Faye Gaines and I were in the area attending a SFTA board meeting, and decided to stop by the Fort as we headed for home. Much to my surprise, the chapel had been moved to the front entrance drive. It was so far removed from its original location that I took it for another chapel, thus drove on by. When I could not find it at the site I remembered, I inquired of an employee on the grounds where it was. One must ask if the converted-relocated chapel retains any historical significance. Perhaps only the beholder can answer.

Returning to the 1993 tour, in Las Animas locating the DAR marker proved to be elusive. Originally placed on the north side of town, it was recently moved to the west side, so stated an article in *Wagon Tracks,* the SFTA quarterly periodical. Twice I drove up and down the main thoroughfare, only to find nothing. However, a small street-corner (pocket) sized park currently being constructed may be the future location of the important marker. That possibility did not help me on this day, and because I had a scant half hour before Boggsville would close, I opted not to track it down.

Boggsville—the last time I visited this once important sheep and cattle center, it was too far gone to even qualify for urban renewal, assuming that someone somewhere wanted to live here. During the interim I knew that the Boggs house had been restored, and as I pulled into the small parking area, the stunning results could be seen a hundred fifty yards distant. There was no sign of life in the locked mobile trailer that served as a visitor center, so I raced down the path to the house, hoping it was still unlocked. Of course, it was not. Peering in the windows, I noticed there was still work to be finished. An inviting porch extended across the full front of the ranch style structure. One could imagine the Boggs family rocking away on a warm summer evening, but I was quickly to learn otherwise.

The Prowers house nearby was a strange sight. Leaning askew with huge braces enclosing its walls, and its roof jacked up several feet above the supporting walls, it appeared as though the slightest movement—even a sneeze—would send what remained of this once elegant structure crashing to the ground in a heap of adobe bricks. One must admire the dedication and determination of the Boggsville Revitalization Committee for undertaking such a formidable project.

As I walked around the house, I realized I was on a marked trail, complete with numbered interpretive markers. Since I entered in mid-trail, I thought I had but two choices. I was soon to learn that the trail contained several loops which doubled back upon themselves. All this would have been made perfectly clear by the map available outside the visitor center which I had failed to pick up earlier in my haste to beat the announced closing hour.

All across the Trail I have been thwarted by closed museums and sites. Initially I faulted myself for the misfortune of being at the right place at the wrong time. But. gradually I have come to realize this was not always so. I was where I should be at the right time, but those in charge of the specific facility were not. Now, it is uncharitable to criticize, for most of these facilities exist solely because of the unswerving dedication of volunteers—persons who do not ask for monetary reward but, instead, feel privileged to engage in this "labor of love." Yet, for those of us who travel great distances for the express purpose of experiencing a special bit of history that has been preserved by those laborers of love, the disappointment of being locked out is profound.

Returning my attention to the outer loop of the Boggsville trail, it borders the Purgatoire River. Suddenly, the occasional mosquito I had noticed for some time became a sting-inflicting squadron. With no one else within miles, all of those critters focused their attention solely on me. With this new-found knowledge, I was not sure how much tranquil rocking was engaged in by the Boggs family on their front porch. I finally was forced to abandon reading the interpretive markers as well as completing the entire trail, and I dashed back to the car, vowing that my next visit would be in December.

Upon reflection, I realize my discomfort was minor when pitted against what the trailers had to endure hour after hour, day in day out, when traveling in mosquito-infested country, which covers much of the eastern half of the Trail. Susan Magoffin minced no words in describing the agony of human and beast. On one particularly unbearable night she said, "their knocking against the carriage *reminded me of a hard rain.*"[6] Because Susan was pampered by her husband and traveled in as grand a style as the prairies would allow, her suffering cannot ever be termed as such when compared with that of those who did not know the comfort of a rockaway carriage by day and a snug tent at night.

Throughout life one often encounters places which warrant revisiting. Such a place is Bent's Old Fort, the much heralded, gigantic private trading post on the Arkansas River in southeast Colorado. As I walked up the long path to those mighty gates, I wondered what new experience would add to my already overflowing memory bank of this impressive structure. A covered wagon was parked outside the gates. I looked beneath it, and, yes, a huge log was lashed to the undercarriage. It was a spare part for the wagon, which was cut from the dense hardwood forest at Council Grove, a standard practice followed by all caravans when they stopped there.

Seeing Tom, the one remaining ox at the Fort, was high on my list this day. However, it was not Tom, but rather, a vain and noisy peacock that first gained my attention as he strutted majestically in the corral, with his gigantic fan spread as wide as he was able for all to see.

Only a few tourists had arrived by the eight a.m. opening, thus

Park Ranger Greg Holt was free to chat at length. Because his costume was that of a nineteenth century trader, I did not immediately associate him with his park service position. Attempting to recreate the spirit of the time when the Fort was a living, breathing institution apparently is important to the NPS. This was also achieved on the tour of the Fort through interactive scenarios Greg conducted with us tourists. At the blacksmith shop—he was the smithy here—he recruited a teenage boy to serve as his apprentice. The lad's job was to man the giant bellows, and whenever his enthusiasm waned Greg urged him on, reminding him that he was expected to keep the fire going ten hours a day, and that his apprenticeship would last a number of years. No blacksmith apprentice recruits came forward that day.

Several times I extricated myself from the group and mounted the bastion, hoping to see Tom in the fields beyond. I finally spotted him grazing near the river. Just before leaving the Fort, I scanned the fields once again, but no Tom. As I exited the gates, there he was twenty feet in front of me. He was solid mahogany in color and much sleeker in body than I had expected. In a most commanding manner he crossed the path and stopped to inspect the skeleton of the Fort's new tepee, glanced up aloofedly at me, and then ambled out into the pasture for more grazing.

From La Junta to Trinidad I would be retracing ground previously covered. My purpose now was to get inside the Baca and Bloom houses, both which were closed on my earlier visit. I had learned from my charming motel hosts in La Junta, who were even more charming than when I first met them three years ago, that the Baca house would be certified as a significant Santa Fe National Historic Trail site by the NPS the next day. With such luck, perhaps I should never again complain when I discover a closed museum.

At the south edge of La Junta I caught my first glimpse of the Spanish Peaks, barely perceptible in the noonday haze. Although they were visible to the naked eye, not so to my camera. The photo I took was a washout, literally. Fifty-five miles farther down the road I snapped the shudder again. The Peaks were now due west of me, at about two o'clock as highway U.S. 350 was heading in a southwesterly direction. Photo results—no better. It may be time to put the old Konica back in mothballs. In another ten to fifteen miles the caravan travelers would find the Peaks over their right shoulders and their landmark would be Fisher's Peak above Raton Pass.

Before reaching this point I had stopped by Iron Spring to see what progress the U.S. Forest Service had made at this, one of three Colorado waysides along the Trail. The parking area was completed, and one limestone post bearing the park service Trail logo had been placed in the ruts. Surveyor flags marked where others would be erected, but no evidence of the proposed interpretive sign was found. The efforts of these two federal agencies to break the Trail out of a century of obscurity and into the conscious awareness of present day America have not been without controversy, as I had learned earlier in Elkhart, Kansas. My impression of this particular site: the parking area may intrude too closely upon the ruts which cut through a fairly flat plain. Even more perplexing was that no attempt was made to tie Iron Spring, the focal point of this site, into the scheme. I was told later that the ranch owner did not wish intrusion on his land. Recalling my first encounter with the "lady of the ranch" and her two young cowboy sons, I found that difficult to believe. I am led to assume that other factors are involved.

I was now hurrying toward Trinidad, concerned whether there would be any room at any inn. This was Santa Fe Trail Festival weekend, a big event for all of southeast Colorado. My third attempt proved successful. Why I even bothered checking the first two cloned franchise motels, I will never know. The small mom and pop operation was clean, economically priced, and but one block from the Baca and Bloom houses. "Pop" was a talker, particularly when he learned I was from Santa Fe. He had lived there for a period, and there he met his wife. When I told him I was traveling the Santa Fe Trail, he reminded me that I was standing at its edge. Main Street in Trinidad *is* the Trail.

Excusing myself from my garrulous host, I walked to the historic houses which were perched side by side on a sharp rise directly above the old Trail. I learned that time would allow me to tour only one this day. However, the admission fee included both. Far be it from me to pay twice. I could wait one day to view the interiors, but could stroll the Victorian gardens of the Bloom house now. The gardens were terraced above the back of the three-story Empire style brick mansion, and proved to be a fine viewing spot of the elegantly adorned structure.

As I walked down the steps toward the house, I saw a figure dressed in period costume seated on a bench in the cool shade of a giant Blue Spruce evergreen tree. I moved closer, but could not discern any movement from the figure who appeared to be reading a book. Was this a living person or a mannequin placed in this idyllic setting to enhance the nineteenth century atmosphere? Was this the young matron of the house, Sarah Thacher Bloom, who found this quiet spot perfect for reading a book of romantic verse? Not until I was but a few feet away did the figure move. She was one of the tour guides, and had selected this spot to rest while waiting for the next group to form.

We both laughed at my confusion, and I joined her on the bench. She was a local teenager on her first job. She said the greatest joy of this position was chatting with the many people who visited the house. There was much to learn about both houses, their owners, and the Santa Fe Trail, but she would have the information mastered in short order, I was sure. Then I glanced at the "book of romantic verse" she was reading. It was Tony Hillerman's latest mystery novel, *The Coyote Speaks.*

By the time the Bloom house was built in 1882, the railroad had replaced the Trail as the primary overland mode of travel. However, its builder, Frank G. Bloom, did travel to the west from Pennsylvania on the Trail, so there is a connection in addition to that of location.

The Baca house enjoys a more direct relation to the Trail, having been built in 1870 by Trail merchant John S. Hough. Its present sobriquet is attributed to the second owners, Felipe and Maria Baca. Building materials and furnishings were transported over the Trail. One can imagine the seven Baca children racing down the long flight of stairs to the Trail below whenever the shout went throughout town that a caravan was approaching. And what of the reaction from those in the train at the sight of such an elegant house so far removed from eastern "civilization"? I am prompted to wonder how many fine private residences from Franklin, Missouri to Santa Fe, New Mexico had a Santa Fe Trail street address.

When I arrived at the Baca house the next morning to witness the certification ceremony, a crowd had already gathered in the placita behind the house, and a mariachi band was providing a musical festive mood. Several familiar faces from the SFTA were there, and I soon met a number of others. A common interest so often creates an instant bond, so I again discovered. Following the ceremony I toured the two houses which, to my delight, were open free of charge in honor of the occasion.

It was now time to think of heading home, for Trinidad was to be the terminus of this particular tour. But, one more site I had to visit, so I headed west on State Highway 12. Marion Russell's grave at Stonewall was my destination. The little cemetery atop a hill overlooking Marion's apple-green valley and the imposing stone wall beyond moved me as deeply this day as on my first visit. This time I planned to drive on through the Stonewall, up through Cucharas Pass, and pass on the west side of the Spanish Peaks.

I drove through the opening in the wall, turned my Cherokee around partway up the hill, drove back through the wall again, and pulled off the highway. Alighting from the car, I walked up to the wall on one side of the highway and as close as an imposing fence would permit on the other. Marion's poetic description of her first encounter with the wall expresses it best. "Suddenly," she wrote, "we came to a gap in the towering wall and drove through a natural gateway. God, it seemed, had decided to let us into the Garden [of Eden]."[7]

Soon after cresting Cucharas Pass the Spanish Peaks hove into view. What a spectacular sight—close enough to touch, so it seemed. Not the distant and often haze-enshrouded target the Trail travelers set their sights on, but two overpowering "rocks" directly before my eyes. What a shame travelers were denied this view. Here, not only did the Peaks' proximity reveal sculptured detail of rock and flora, but they seemed to extend their broad flanks in protective embrace. And so, with my eyes riveted on these wondrous gifts from Mother Earth, I closed another chapter of my wanderings along the Santa Fe Trail.

Note: Several years later I again came under the spell of the Huajatollas, the Ute Indian name by which the Spanish Peaks are known. I was driving on U.S. 160 west of Walsenburg, Colorado. Here they are to the south. They easily dominate all about them, hovering above an expansive, fertile valley of such beauty that even Roget's *Thesaurus* is of no help. Powerful and majestic. No, I think not, but rather graceful and serene. Had this been the Road to Santa Fe, I fear very few would have reached their intended destination.

Fast forward to 2002 when I again was in western Kansas, attending the "6 Western Chapters Gathering" hosted by Wagon Bed Spring chapter of SFTA. This was our third such annual event. Several years earlier it occurred to me that the local SFTA chapters were scheduling fantastic tours, events many of the rest of us would love to attend. However, the distance to most was too great for a single day excursion, although passionately dedicated trailers such as Jesse Scott and Mike Slater would turn up regularly at chapter meetings and field trips, many often hundreds of miles from their respective homes.

Wondering out loud at a Cimarron Cutoff chapter meeting about this same time period, I questioned if there might be any interest in gathering the six western chapters on a weekend to tour local trail sites. Without much discussion, the decision was a resounding "yes," and the Clayton group promptly offered to host the inaugural event, and Sue Richardson agreed to organize it. That was 2000, and thus began an exciting and enlightening series of informal chapter-organized gatherings stretching from Ulysses, Kansas to Santa Fe. In 2001 Bent's Fort chapter was host.

Jeff Trotman, president of the Wagon Bed Spring chapter, was our adroit Wagonmaster for the third two-day tour, in 2002, which began north of Fort Aubry on the Mountain Route and terminated on the Cimarron Cutoff at Point of Rocks/Middle Spring in the Cimarron National Grassland, literally in Kansas' southwest corner.

The Fort Aubry site is in a pasture on private property. The owner and the cattle, the latter which were pastured nearby, graciously allowed us access. Of course, the cattle stared and stared at us with their big brown eyes and those long, sweeping lashes. Oh, how I envy those lashes. Nothing beyond depressions in the ground remain of Fort Aubry, and although its military tenure lasted but a year, its name still resonates with Trail buffs. Francis X. Aubry, "Skimmer of the Plains," was fixated with speed, and determined to cut his time from each succeeding trip between Independence and Santa Fe. On September 17, 1848 he achieved the ultimate speed record when he struggled into Independence five days and sixteen hours after leaving Santa Fe.[8] I suppose one must admire his fortitude, but I dwell more on the animals he rode to death in the process. More interesting to me is Marion Russell's friendship with Aubry. He led the train that transported Marion at age seven and her family to Santa Fe on her first of five Trail trips in 1852. Aubry was an "ardent admirer" of Marion's mother, thus he showered special attention on the young girl and her brother, Will. Throughout the voyage she speaks glowingly of Aubry.

Several miles east of the fort, the Aubry Cutoff heads south where it eventually joins the Cimarron Cutoff near Flag Spring in Oklahoma. Would that time had permitted us to walk the pristine ruts that stretch roughly four miles south of the Arkansas River. Yet, we were not denied the opportunity over the next two days to experience miles of swales on this parched western Kansas prairie, and we did not have long to wait. Fine Mountain Route ruts were visible just across a fence along our dirt road route to Indian Mound.

Jeff was determined that we see almost every DAR marker in western Kansas, and that we did. He had created an excellent handbook describing and locating the sites that we visited. One description he wrote particularly amused me, this being the text describing DAR marker #96. It reads: "We have no interesting tales about the [Kansas] State Line marker." He then proceeded to explain in a rather lengthy paragraph a most engaging "tale" of the marker's history, which included several relocations and an adventurous hike to its present "home."

To view the marker at Indian Mound (an estimated 18 miles east of Fort Aubry), which traders named Chouteau's Mound, a climb up the short but steep hill was necessary. "Leave the snakes alone!" he shouted, and he got no argument from me. The little protuberance sits all alone on a level, featureless plain. From the summit one can gaze at the nearby Arkansas River, where a small island, Chouteau's Island, once stood before the river insisted on having its way. The story goes that in 1816 Auguste Chouteau and a band of trappers sought refuge on the island when they were attacked by Indians. Hence, its name.

Five miles east was Lakin, home to two of SFTA's most esteemed members: Paul Bentrup and Pat Heath.

Following lunch at the Kearny County Museum, an exceptional facility which Pat has passionately and efficiently directed for many years, we headed south across the Arkansas River—known as the Upper Crossing—and were now on the Cimarron Cutoff. The Kearny County sand hills, their traversing which caused the travelers so much misery, were visible to the west. Yet at least one diarist, George C. Sibley, saw more than misery in these hills when he wrote in his journal during the 1825 Santa Fe Trail survey, which he directed, "[f]rom the High Ridges I could see the Sand Hills.... These when the sun shone bright on them looked like so many Pillars of fire."[9]

I was not prepared for the drama of the Menno Road Ruts on the south edge of the sand hills. At least five distinct swales were spread out both north and south from the road. A hint of green in the midst of the current drought was a surprise. What a perfect spot for SFTA's Trail crossing markers, but none existed. More ruts: Higgs, Klien, Joyce, Deyce. I had no idea so many jewels existed around Ulysses. The map supplement to the NPS Santa Fe National Historic Trail "Comprehensive Management and Use Plan" (1990) does not indicate that any of these are extant ruts. It is time this be updated. By now the heat was raging above 100 degrees, and we occasionally thought we could relate to the misery the original travelers experienced along this road. Yet, as we escaped to the comfort of our air-conditioned vehicles, and downed refreshing iced water, that was pure myth.

South of Ulysses is famous Wagon Bed Spring. Not much had changed since my earlier visits except for the hog farms that were dotted over the countryside for miles in all directions. There has been much opposition to these farms, particularly the unbearable stench wafting from them which the NPS believes compromises the visitors' experience to the site. (Even as I write this, I can sensually recall that terrible odor, such is the power of the human olfactory sense.) That may be unpleasant, but more depressing are the deplorable conditions the hogs are forced to suffer. Not all buildings have windows, although I have been told the buildings contain a circulating air system. But where is the sunlight? Such cruelty.

The next day our caravan again snaked across section line roads searching out more ruts. My attention was riveted to the prospect of seeing "False Point of Rocks." Jeff refused to reveal where or what this mysterious site was. As we pulled onto the east boundary of Cimarron National Grassland aiming for Middle Spring, it became apparent that the counterfeit Point was nearby. And, indeed, it was. Although much smaller than the original, it would have been possible for novice travelers to mistake it for the real thing. Yet, they had not yet arrived at Middle Spring, which was the first of the two sites approached from the east, so why the mix-up? Jeff had no explanation. There is no modern signage to mark this spot, and although I unsuccessfully scanned the landscape in all directions for some semblance of a landmark for future reference, I must wonder if I will recognize it on my next trip to this famous site.

By the time we reached Middle Spring, the box lunches awaiting us were welcome, indeed. We lounged under a green canopy of trees, a stark contrast from the "treeless and muddy water hole,"[10] which was often its condition when the wagon trains rolled up to the Spring . Yet, the extremely low level of the pond in the face of the present drought may not have been too different from then. As on previous visits, our next stop following lunch was to the Point of Rocks summit. Three states—Kansas, Oklahoma, Colorado, and possibly New Mexico—are easily visible from that windy brow.

It is not possible to experience the Point and Spring too often. I have visited both in a variety of climatic conditions, all which were usually accompanied by wind. Even a frosty cold March wind Faye Gaines and I faced a few years previously was not "mean" enough to force us to retreat to the comfort of our heated vehicle as we lunched. Did we think we had a point to make? Our 6 Western Chapters odyssey had come to an end all too quickly, and each of us took our separate paths home, but not without commitment to gather in another year at the "end of the trail" in Santa Fe.

Over the years there have been many opportunities to re-visit a few sites when travelling to and from Kansas, sometimes visiting family and friends, other times attending SFTA events. One such re-visit occurred on the drive home from the 2011 Symposium (yes, another "fast forward") in Dodge City. The Symposium concluded on a brisk yet sunny Sunday morning with a delicious cowboy breakfast, served up with biscuits and gravy, sausage, and lots of hot cowboy coffee, followed by a brief church service held at Boothill Museum ruts nine miles west of town. Faye Gaines was again my passenger, and, as always, was amenable to whatever adventures the Gods had on the agenda for us. We decided to head west, with Charlie's Ruts at Deerfield, KS our first stop. Yes, these ruts are still quite prominent, having been well preserved by Charlie's son, the late Paul Bentrup, previously noted as a leading SFTA founder ("character" may be a more accurate adjective, for there never was an occasion when Paul did not have some jocular remark to share with the audience he always had gathered around him) and authority on this section of the Trail. On this particular visit, a small herd of horses guarded the ruts. Although the severe drought encasing western Kansas had stripped all vegetation from the soil, pristine swales could still be seen.

A few miles farther west we entered Lakin, home of the late Pat Heath. We drove by the outstanding museum she directed for years. It was closed, as I expected, a situation I had all too frequently encountered over the years. However, much to my delight, the twelve-sided barn from a neighborhood farm she had worked so diligently to save was now installed on the museum grounds.

From Lakin we crossed the Arkansas River—dry, of course—and headed south toward Ulysses, aiming for more ruts. First on our route were the outstanding five abreast Menno Ruts. This time we were spared the 100+ degree temperature and blasting hot winds which we endured during the 2002 6 Western Chapters gathering. As I had noted before, there are still no Santa Fe National Historic Trail crossing signs to identify the swales that cross the dirt track we were on. Considering the large number of signs spread across the length of the Trail, I fail to understand why these ruts have been ignored and are still unmarked.

A few miles farther south on Kansas Highway 25 we took a dirt track west to Wagon Bed Spring, en route being forced to navigate around a herd of curious cows. The Spring site is well tended by Wagon Bed Spring chapter of the SFTA. We identified more ruts than

I remembered from previous visits, including one set perpendicular to the others, the latter aiming in the correct direction, the former not so, in my view. Surprisingly, considering the extreme drought affecting the southwest, spring water was trickling through the wagon bed. A metal full-size silhouette buffalo had been added to the site.

Returning to the highway, we stopped at the nearby Jedediah Smith interpretive overlook. A short distance from the overlook we came upon another directional marker to the Spring, this approach being from the south. This was new to me, so we turned onto the dirt track which took us back to the cows and then to the Spring.

The final treat of this idyllic day came at Faye's ranch. We drove into her pasture where numerous bands of ruts stretched as far as the eye could see. The pasture was literally covered with ribbons of ruts coursing south of Faye's house and Point of Rocks, heading toward the Sangre de Cristo mountains in the west. I have known Faye for over twenty years, and have visited the Point almost as many times, yet this was the first occasion I had to visit these ruts. They certainly were worth the wait. What a perfect ending to "Picking up Loose Threads."

Notes

1. Chadwick, Douglas. The American Prairie. *National Geographic,* 1993, 184(4), pg. 99.

2. Russell, Marion Sloan. *Land of Enchantment: Memoirs of Marion Russell Along the Santa Fe Trail as Dictated to Mrs. Hal Russell.* Albuquerque, New Mexico: University of New Mexico Press, 1981, p. 105.

3. Lavender, David. *Bent's Fort.* Lincoln, Nebraska: University of Nebraska Press, 1954, p. 340.

4. Vestal, Stanley. *The Old Santa Fe Trail.* Boston, Massachusetts: Houghton Mifflin, 1939.

5. The fort over its brief life was known by three names. Its original name was Fort Fauntleroy for a Colonel Thomas Fauntleroy, then Fort Wise for Virginia governor Henry A. Wise, and finally Fort Lyon for Brigadier General Nathaniel Lyon.

6. Drumm, Stella M. (Ed.). *Down the Santa Fe Trail and Into Mexico: The Diary of Susan Shelby Magoffin, 1846-1847.* Lincoln, Nebraska: University of Nebraska Press, 1982, p. 34.

7. Russell, *op. cit.*, p. 129

8. Barry, Louise. *The Beginning of the West: Annals of the Kansas Gateway to the American West 1540–1854.* Topeka, Kansas: Kansas State Historical Society, 1972, pgs. 775-6

9. Gregg, Kate L. *The Road to Santa Fe: The Journal and Diaries of George Champlin Sibley.* Albuquerque, New Mexico: University of New Mexico Press, 1952, p. 76.

10. "Like a Ribbon Across the Prairie," Cimarron, Kiowa and Comanche National Grasslands brochure.

Middle Spring, Kansas.

Point of Rocks, Kansas.

Boggs house, Boggsville, Colorado.

Bloom house, Trinidad, Colorado.

False Point of Rocks, Cimarron Grasslands, Kansas.

6

Floating Across Missouri

1993 was the year I planned to complete my sojourn along the Santa Fe Trail by exploring the Missouri section, that being the easternmost stretch—the beginning. Specifically, mid-September was the time period I had selected because the chances of encountering the heat and humidity of summer and the unpredictability of spring and winter were lessened. But, this was 1993, the year of the great 500-year flood which inundated a good portion of the Midwest. Yet, I could no longer contain the urge to hit the trail, and since the Missouri River was now well within its banks, I aimed my Cherokee for Franklin, Missouri, the head of the Trail.

My first stops were in Wichita and Leawood, Kansas for brief visits with family and friends. By now, they all were familiar with my on-the-fly visits en route to another date with history. As I battled the rush hour traffic around Kansas City, I smiled at the incongruity of charging down this expressway, with all of its eight or more lanes a sea of high powered vehicles, on my way to a tiny road that for a brief moment in history over a hundred seventy years ago was thrust into fame like the pavement beneath me never would experience. Not surprisingly, my thoughts turned to that mysterious concept, "time." How could I ever come to any understanding of its meaning with one foot stuck in the Santa Fe Trail of the nineteenth century while the other was speeding into the twenty-first. Yet, perhaps this very antithesis is what we must experience to understand that "time" is not a singular concept. Most important of all, we must understand that "time" is not a mechanical clock on the wall, but rather, a series of events linked together by an inner sense and need for continuity that knows nothing of that clock or the separation between the events.

Pondering this imponderable while staying alert to the racing vehicles around me, I noticed a large object in the sky directly in front of me, perhaps a hundred feet above the ground. As the distance between us diminished I ruled out helicopter and hot air balloon. By then its shape and identifying markings were visible. It was the blimp Shamu, headed for some athletic event at Kansas City's Truman Complex. No matter what its actual mission, for me Shamu was coming to meet the past, and from that elevation it would be able to see any ruts that still might scour the Missouri countryside.

I spent the night in Boonville, and early the next morning I headed across the bridge that spans the Missouri River and into the bustle of flood cleanup. As I crossed that narrow bridge with its metal grid flooring, my mind went back to another time—or rather numerous times—when that bridge carried first me between my home in Indiana and college in Kansas, and later when Bill and I lived in Ohio and later in Indiana, back to Kansas to visit his family. My Uncle Alvin drove it once and announced, never again, primarily due to that metal grid flooring. Of all the bridges I have crossed in my lifetime, none conjures up such vivid memories as does the one at Boonville.

As I drove down the ramp, I immediately spotted the DAR marker that still stands at the intersection of State Highways 5 and 87. First reports we in Santa Fe had received from the flood site were that it too, along with all the plaques that mark the trailhead at Old Franklin, had been swept downstream. Could those dedicated DAR members have foreseen such a disaster when they selected solid granite markers set on equally solid stone foundations? A layer of silt partly covered the foundation, but that was all. Immediately behind the marker loomed the flooded remnant of what I presumed was the Kit Carson motel.

Highway 87 leads to the Old Franklin site, but not on this day. The road had washed away and was closed to both vehicular and pedestrian traffic. I walked to the barricade and looked out over huge pools of water extending several miles back from the river's banks. Back at the DAR marker, a workman pointed out the unimproved road to Rivercene and confirmed that it was passable. A fresh load of gravel had been spread up to the mansion's drive only the day before.

I stopped at the entrance to the drive, stepped from my Jeep, and stared up toward the three story historic Victorian structure with a center turret standing prominently against a mansard roof. Everything about it looked gray and dingy. I was reminded of the scene in "Gone With the Wind" when Scarlett returned to Tara from Atlanta during the Civil War. At first she could see nothing at the end of the long lane. Then the moon broke through the clouds, and there it stood, gray and dingy. But it stood. And so did Rivercene.

The mansion was built in the mid 1860s by an affluent riverboat tycoon, Captain Joseph Kinney, who spared no expense to create the most elegant house for its day in western Missouri.

As I gazed first at the house and then at the four acres of dried mud that surrounded it, a woman emerged from the house. I walked up the long circular driveway and there met Jody Lenz and her jolly Westminster terrier. I mounted the six steps to the broad porch, noticing that only the top third of the railing still stood. The water had reached three and a half feet into the first floor—roughly eight feet from the ground—Jody said. She invited me inside to see both the ugly and beautiful that Rivercene was on this particular day in September of 1993.

Ladders, buckets, cleaning compounds, and all the other "accoutrements" required for serious cleaning were lined up in the middle of the floor in each room. In the grand living room, which boasted one of the house's nine Italian marble fireplaces, stood a huge square grand piano, a possession of the original owner. Because its weight precluded moving it during the flood, this magnificent instrument sat out the deluge atop four metal folding chairs. How they bore the weight, I cannot imagine.

Although all the interior walls showed the ravages of flood mud, the abundance of wood molding, doors, and hand carved mahogany gleamed. The three cleanings Jody and husband Ron applied, miraculously restored them almost to their original splendor. Not so the kitchen cabinets of recent vintage which had disintegrated. Much work was still to be done—twenty students from the University of Missouri would arrive soon to help demud—and it was apparent that their efforts would succeed. And to think, only last May restoration efforts had progressed sufficiently for the Lenz' to open Rivercene as a bed and breakfast. What courage and inherent strength they possess to be able to pick up the pieces and start over again. No, this was worse than starting over. Is this not similar to the character and spirit we attribute to all those pioneers who settled this country? Like the Santa Fe Trail, that spirit lives on, and I found it embodied in Jody and Ron Lenz.

Realizing I was keeping Jody from her work, I thanked her, wished her well, and turned to leave. At the bottom of the porch steps, flanking the non-existing balusters, were several newly planted chrysanthemums, sending forth tiny rays of color amid all that grizzly gray. She simply had to have some color, Jody said, to keep her spirits high.

I drove away to my next stop—New Franklin. When Old Franklin finally succumbed to the Missouri River in 1828 after two disastrous floods in three years, its residents built a new town several miles away on high ground. They chose wisely this time, for New Franklin has been dry through all the river's violent upheavals.

Traffic increased significantly as I pulled into town. Today New Franklin was celebrating Santa Fe Trail Days. Eventually, I found a parking place several blocks from the one business street, where a crafts fair was underway. There were several sites and markers to visit so I set out to find them, spending only a few scant minutes perusing the booths spread out along the sidewalk. I found the only surviving building from Old Franklin, a neat two story white painted brick house originally known as the Franklin Academy. It appeared to have survived its journey quite well. Later I learned that there was doubt that this building ever stood in Old Franklin, and that the genuine Academy remained on its original foundation until 1923 when it was razed.[1]

Having learned that I could get to Boone's Lick State Park and several Trail sites by taking the back roads, I prevailed upon a policeman handling traffic control at the Santa Fe Trail Days for directions. Hardly had he started his verbal directions with much gesturing than he realized a written diagram was needed. However, even that did not satisfy him at first, so he crumbled the paper and started again. As it turned out, not to worry, because this back gravel road, being the only road not flooded in the area, was now the main road to Boonville and beyond, and thus was quite heavily traveled.

Today all traffic was headed for the festival at New Franklin, and everyone was hurrying to the parade, which was due to commence shortly. Four or five trucks hauling horse trailers were included in this unscheduled parade, obviously to be part of the real parade. And what was bringing up the rear but the featured attraction—a mule-drawn Conestoga wagon followed by several buggies. The occupants of all were dressed in period costumes.

On down the road I passed through Franklin. Just how many Franklins exist, I queried to myself. At last count, three. Old Franklin was the first, and it was from here that William Becknell set out in 1821 for his great adventure to Santa Fe. Then we have New Franklin, founded in 1828. Finally, "just plain" Franklin, which came into being in 1912 when a group of irate New Franklin residents seceded over a disagreement with the political powers and formed a new town. I thank H. Denny Davis for pulling all the facts together and helping me make sense of all those Franklins. Davis suggested in the referenced *Wagon Tracks* article above that the Trail-trekker avoid the modern town of Franklin, but such was not possible this day if I wished to see the few sites in Boone's Lick Country that still could be reached. Anyway, the sleepy little town held a certain charm even without a historically significant past.

Continuing my drive down the road—State Highway Z—I noticed a huge clump of flood debris clinging to a power line overhead, indicating how shockingly high were the floodwaters in this area. It was a reminder of the Ohio River flood I experienced as a child many years ago. Just beyond, I came upon another DAR marker. It was in the front yard of Cedar Grove, the first of a number of fine nineteenth century antebellum dwellings I would see that attest to the affluence Boone's Lick Country has known since early settlement days. According to the Franklin area historic sites brochure, this is probably the only still standing example of an attached Federal and Greek Revival house in Missouri. The Federal house was built in 1824, and was a silent witness to many caravans bound for Santa Fe which lumbered down the Trail—the highway I was now travelling—just beyond its low stone wall.

The next DAR marker on my route was at the Cooper's Fort site, one of a number of private forts built to protect the early settlers. It was in the middle of flooded lands and still closed to vehicular traffic, according to my last report. However, no barricade blocked the dirt road leading to the site, thus I turned onto it. The ground as far as the eye could see was covered with that ugly gray flood mud. Very quickly small ponds of water appeared on both sides of the road. Then I was driving through shallow mud puddles, and finally much larger and deeper ones which I chose not to cross. Perhaps I could have walked to the site, although it was not visible from where I stopped, but elected to heed the advice received, and turned around.

Boone's Lick State Park was my next port of call. The small park with a trail leading down to the salt spring was well maintained. However, the thick woods and undergrowth indigenous to the area was somewhat unsettling for its isolation, and uncomfortable for its humidity. Salt-making was the major industry here in the early nineteenth century, and just about everyone, including Becknell, worked at the "lick" at some time or other.

My next destination was Arrow Rock State Historic Site, which sits directly across the river from this park. Although Becknell was able to cross the river at this spot, I could not. A ferry, which operated for 116 years, carried his little troop across. However, it ceased operating in 1927, and no bridge has replaced it. Thus, I had to retrace my steps in part and cross the Boonville bridge again. But, the road I was following was by no means boring, and I was treated to a scenic drive across ridgetops and down into wooded gullies of solid greenery. I was struck by the lovely houses that dotted the countryside, and I wondered what provided the owners with such a comfortable life style. There were no crops—the terrain was too hilly—and no livestock was visible in the green pastures. Oh, I did see four piglets gamboling in the middle of the road, whom I sternly shooed to their nearby pen.

This could not be a gentrified outskirts of a nearby city because none existed. In 1863 when Joseph Pratt Allyn crossed the area by railroad, preparatory to embarking upon the road to Santa Fe, he too observed the prosperous appearance of the countryside, and noted this in his diary, *West by Southwest*.[2] All the way into Independence I would notice the appearance of affluence, from modern brick ranch style houses to elegant antebellum mini-mansions, many flying American flags although this was no holiday. Whatever provided the monetary means to construct these lovely structures has been in full sway for over a hundred years.

As I snaked my way up the hill on the back road to New Franklin, I once again passed those horse trailers, this time returning from the parade, with their cargoes lustily munching on well earned oats following their hard work entertaining parade viewers. Where were the Conestoga wagon and buggies? On Broadway, giving the folks rides. Reluctantly, I drove directly through the town, noting that it was well past one p.m., and Arrow Rock was calling. As I write these words, I regret that I allowed myself to be a captive of time. I am convinced that some priceless experiences awaited me at Santa Fe Trail Day which, sadly, I chose to pass up.

Back in Boonville I sought out Harley Park located on a prominence overlooking the river, beyond which was, supposedly, the Santa Fe trailhead. The route passed through a flooded-out residential district, quite conspicuous by the huge piles of rubbish stacked at the curb. Halfway up a hill to the park, a section of the street was washed out producing a menacing looking gully which would have been too much of a challenge even for my Cherokee. Should I continue on foot? Not knowing the distance and with my eye on the speeding clock, I settled for a view halfway up the hill. The only difference, I surmised, was that at the hilltop overlook I could have seen *more* water than my present view exposed.

Twenty minutes after leaving Boonville I was being ushered to my table at the Old Tavern in Arrow Rock. I had not missed the noon serving, although only four other guests were also partaking of a late luncheon. Arrow Rock is a national historic landmark, and all the stunning period houses I had passed coming into town are occupied, some as antique or gift shops, others as bed and breakfasts, and still others simply as private residences. It is a low key Williamsburg, not as well known as its Virginia cousin, but every bit as authentic and charming, exuding the aura of a by-gone era. The old tavern was built by Joseph Huston in 1834, the period when Independence's star was rapidly ascending as the trailhead of the roads west while Arrow Rock's was descending. Yet, it is certain that more than a few Santa Fe traders partook of a meal and spent the night under the roof of this hostel or on the lawn surrounding it.

The dining room was bright and airy with banks of windows on two sides. The colonial furnishings were set off with brass chandeliers and lace tier curtains. Perusing the menu required no cogitation, and I settled on a sugar-cured ham on a Kaiser bun with a side of the Tavern's famous cole slaw. I was not disappointed. Before leaving the Tavern, I roamed about the first floor. It was also furnished with authentic nineteenth century period pieces. After but one hour in Arrow Rock, and that spent exclusively in one dwelling, I had already formed the opinion that the millions of people in the U.S. who have not visited this tiny slice of Americana have missed an enriching and broadening experience.

Following this tasty repast, I strolled the streets for a closer look at the houses and shops, entering most that were open for business. It was too late in the day to join a guided tour, so again I found myself making a mental note to return sometime in the future during the regular tourist season. At the Visitors Center I chatted with superintendent Mike Dickey about the recent flood. Arrow Rock is located atop a high bluff, thus was not threatened, although it was without water for several days. Mike showed me photos of Old Franklin, pointing out where the important Trail landmarks were—all under water, of course. Having seen enough of flood waters for one day, I repaired to the theatre to view the interpretive film. The theatre walls were adorned with a most interesting map of the Santa Fe Trail. Numerous important sites were highlighted by quotations of travelers who had been there and had penned their impressions. Beside each quotation was a photo or sketch of the author. Mike explained that the museum was not yet fully furnished, but the exhibits that were in place indicated real promise for the finished product.

My next stop in town was the Big Spring, also known as Santa Fe

Spring. It was here the caravans quenched their thirst and reassembled after ferrying across the river. Then they began the long, steep pull up to the town proper, a very short drive for me this day on a smooth blacktop road.

Spring water no longer issues directly from the ground, but instead is delivered through a pipe over which a neat picnic-style shelter is spread. "Park" is the best description of the spring today. The area around the shelter has been planted with grass, and a small footbridge crosses the stream that receives water from the spring. I could not imagine that this picture bore any resemblance to the area as it was when the wagon trains arrived from the river landing. Present-day Trail purists could not believe that integrity has been maintained at Santa Fe Spring, and as attractive as I found the setting, I must agree.

It was time to move on to the sites between Arrow Rock and Marshall, my destination for the night. I headed for Prairie Park, a magnificent pre-Civil War mansion five miles away. What a marvelous example of southern architecture was this fully restored dwelling. I had to be content, however, to view it from the end of a long walkway and from behind a white picket fence. It was built by William B. Sappington, son of the great physician, Dr. John Sappington, who discovered quinine as a treatment for malaria. Dr. Sappington's pills accompanied the pioneers across the west, and it is safe to say that many a traveler owed his life to this gentle humanitarian.

Pioneer cemeteries have long held a fascination for me, the origin of which time has long since obliterated from my memory. However, one experience does stand out, and this from my Lawrence, Kansas days. Bill and I hoped to buy a few acres of land several miles south of town. Located in a far corner of the plot was a tiny family cemetery dating back to the nineteenth century. This wee page out of the past must be preserved, and I was convinced that no one but me would do so. It certainly had received no attention for a very long time. When we learned that the property had been bought out from under us, I was furious. Whenever I see a long-neglected old cemetery, I think of that small plot of ground in Lawrence whose tender loving care was denied me.

The cemetery I drove up to this day bore no resemblance to the other. It was the Sappington cemetery, a state historic site. In addition to family members, three Missouri governors are buried here, including Meredith Miles Marmaduke, who was also a Santa Fe trader and son-in-law of Dr. John. The cemetery, dotted with opulent marble monuments, was well maintained and the picture of neatness. Even the inscriptions on the oldest tombstones, which had been standing well over one hundred years, were readable. This cemetery was yet another testimony to the prosperity of Boone's Lick Country.

As I retraced my route back to the highway, I once again passed Prairie Park. A short distance beyond, a vintage model Ford in mint condition passed me, heading in the opposite direction. We exchanged the ritualistic waves, a common practice in the rural Midwest. I immediately surmised that he was headed for Prairie Park, and a glance in the rear view mirror confirmed my hunch. Returning to the basic mode of transportation in the nineteenth century may not be practical for the present occupants of Dr. John's son's house, but an old Ford would do just as well.

Note: On yet another occasion, the 2009 SFTA Symposium, a reception was held the evening before the official conference opening on the spacious lawn at Prairie Park. In addition to the abundant finger food spread about and folk music provided by talented SFTA members and locals, a tour of this magnificent house was provided. When we arrived, the line into the house was quite long, so we decided to eat first. As these things usually happen, I became engrossed in interesting conversations, including with a family who lived not far from my former home in Lawrence. Thus, as dusk descended and people began to leave, I thought the opportunity to view the house had evaporated. Not so said a couple with whom I was chatting, Day and Whitney Kerr, much to my surprise the Prairie Park owners. Thus it was that Faye and I received a private, personal tour of this stunning antebellum mansion from the couple who know it best. Complete darkness greeted us as we exited the house much later. Whitney grabbed a flashlight and led us through the night to my Jeep across an equally dark pasture. And so ended yet another incredible experience to add to my expansive Trail memoirs.

Back on Missouri Highway 41, and back to 1993, the next stop was Chestnut Hill, a spacious white clapboard house built in 1844 by yet another Santa Fe trader, Phillip Thompson. Perched high on a bank, it was barely visible from the road. I viewed it as best as possible from the driveway entrance, having rejected the idea of climbing the weed-choked perpendicular bank on the opposite side, and drove on. Only later did I carefully read the guidebooks to discover that faint ruts were located behind the house. Three additional traces were also missed between this point and Marshall. No matter how extensive is my research before embarking on these excursions, I always miss something. On the positive side, what better excuse to return some later day.

In reality, bypassing some sites is due primarily to the enormity of all that is the Santa Fe Trail. Sometimes, even a small segment cannot be totally comprehended in one viewing. Strange though it may seem, continuity is sometimes achieved by passing over some sites so that direct linkage can be achieved between others. This is especially true in Kansas City as I previously have discovered and would reconfirm in a day or two. For example, the houses of Alexander Majors and William Bent need not be visited in the order they appear geographically or in a guidebook to be appreciated for their significance to the Trail. One can drop in and out along the Trail at almost any point, as I have done since embarking on my first Trail trip, and find meaning in the experience and understanding of the road.

To reach the site of Isaac Neff's tavern, I had to drive down yet another gravel road. The tavern was a popular stop-over for caravans headed for Santa Fe. I must wonder how many traders lost a day of travel, if not more, in so doing. I drove into the driveway of the brick bungalow with its farm buildings spread out behind, noticing a stone structure to the left which I assumed was the smokehouse, the only building extant from the original complex. I drove to the back of the house where three people were enjoying "Happy Hour" on an open porch, But, it was a footed bathtub around and upon which a group of kittens were frolicking that caught my attention. At first glance it looked as though the people were relaxing in the tub, and I was not sure if it was proper for me to intrude. Finally realizing that they were seated *behind* the tub, I approached and introduced myself and stated my mission. Yes, the lady confirmed that the stone building was the original smokehouse. I asked if they had ever seen any ruts here or behind the Neff family cemetery, a short distance down the road. No, one of the men replied, but, he encouraged me to visit the cemetery nonetheless, since he had spent much time mowing it.

They offered me several kittens—as many as I desired—but not pecans from the numerous trees that surrounded the property because they had not yet ripened. In response to my surprise at the number and size of the trees, the lady informed me that she had no idea the age of the grove, only that it had been there for many years, and that the largest tree was visible from Marshall, five miles away. Pecan trees are exceedingly long-lived, three hundred years not being unusual. Had I known then how to gauge a pecan tree's age—one foot diameter per one hundred years—I would have taken the measurement of that patriarch which towered above all around it.[3] I was awed by the grove, but not tempted to take a kitten or two, so I bade them goodbye. As I drove away I broke into a broad smile over this encounter with those laid-back folks and their bathtub.

A quarter of a mile farther down the road I came upon the Neff family cemetery, a prime example of a burying plot that had suffered neglect for many years. But, thanks to one of the fellows back at the bathtub, the weeds had been brought under control. It was a dark, dank place, deeply shaded by the many trees that covered the grounds. Many tombstones were damaged, missing, or had tumbled from their foundations, but I was able to piece together a bit of the Neff family genealogy from what remained. I could not detect evidence of ruts which purportedly were in the field behind the cemetery, but in early spring before vegetative growth consumes it all, they may reveal themselves.

Back on the highway, it was but a few miles to Marshall. At the edge of town I looked back over the route I had driven, hoping it was possible to see the majestic pecan tree towering over all, but was disappointed that nothing so obvious appeared on the horizon.

Over dinner I reflected on the day's activities, and was amazed that I had achieved my goal to make it to Marshall the first day. My next assignment was to re-read and organize the next day's journey. Unfortunately, I did not take the time to read the route I had just followed, otherwise I would have discovered several sets of ruts on the outskirts of Marshall that I had missed. The next morning dawned extremely gray, as per the forecast, and for the first 1½ hours the sky was unchanging. In that period I located five DAR markers and a wonderful set of ruts located in the Grand Pass cemetery. These were the first ruts I had seen on this particular journey, so I lingered quite awhile, walking up and down the swales, avoiding grave sites, gazing first in one direction and then in the other. Had the citizens of Grand Pass chosen some other plot to bury their dead, it is doubtful this remnant of the Trail would have survived.

When I stopped at one of a number of fruit stands dotting this section of the state, I noticed that the sky had turned an ominous black and the wind had quickened. I quickly loaded the apples and jam I had purchased into the Cherokee and headed for Dover. By the time I arrived in this hamlet the rain was coming down in torrents. Since there would be no strolling about examining DAR markers or Trail sites, this seemed as good a time as any to stop and plan the rest of the day's route. Forty-five minutes later the rain had not abated, and I discovered I had another problem—water from an unknown source was flooding the floorboard beneath me. Fortunately, I always carry several towels in the car, so for the remainder of that rainy day I sponged water into the towels, wrung them out, and started the process over again.

While sitting out the storm in Dover, I had ample time to compare my plight with that of Trail travelers when they were caught in inclement weather, and they all were. Rarely was it possible to seek shelter in a wagon, for all were filled with cargo, although Josiah Gregg managed to wriggle on top of a tier of boxes and bales during a particularly severe night storm. (Later, I would recall Gregg's continuing account of that same storm. It persisted for forty-eight hours without letup.) Lewis Garrard also wrote of his experiences in rain. "Riding in a wet saddle," he bemoaned, "in rain-saturated clothes, and inhaling the steam from our clammy, unpleasant animals caused feelings most undesirable."[4] Well, my clothes were dry, my saddle wasn't wet, and my animal didn't smell bad. How could I complain?

Eventually, I drove on to my next destination, Lexington, having been forced to pass up Tabo Creek crossing because high water covered portions of the lane leading down to the creek. The creeks I had been crossing since leaving Dover were now raging torrents, in some places spilling out from their banks after having only recently receded from the original flood two months ago.

Lexington, with its many fine old homes and historically significant business district, seemed a good place for a walking tour in my original plan. However, with a steady rain still enshrouding it all, I elected to see what I could from the comfort of my Cherokee. A cannon ball lodged in a column of the courthouse during the Civil War Battle of Lexington was clearly visible from the street as I circled the square, as were several historical markers. I identified the sites of no-longer standing offices of the famous Russell, Majors, and Waddell freighting firm and the merchant and banker Aull Brothers, all well known figures to those who plied the Santa Fe trade. Unfortunately, the buildings that replaced the originals possessed no outstanding architectural style or grace. A fine metal plaque honoring Russell, et al, was located behind the city hospital near the service entrance. Being surrounded by too many trees with low hanging branches and too many robust shrubs, it could easily be missed if one did not know its location. Why such a fine work of art was placed in this remote spot, is a mystery to me.

Lexington boasts one of the four Madonna of the Trail sculptures spread along the Santa Fe Trail, resting in a tiny park on the bluff above the Missouri River. As I pulled to the curb the heavens opened once more, and again I elected to view this splendid work from my Cherokee, excepting for the brief time required to take a photo. However, not even the dense gray sky that engulfed it could diminish the emotion I always experience when in the presence of this lady with her two children. It is the contrast of those heavy boots and the flower bedecked sunbonnet she is wearing that affects me so strongly. Granted, she is not smiling, but there is no somber, downtrodden facial expression that is so typical of photos of nineteenth century folks.

I drove down the bluff aiming for the site of Simpson's Santa Fe

Trail Spring, only to be stopped by a sign warning of high water. This road, Missouri Highway 224, parallels the river for seven miles to the next town, Wellington. Having been under water during the recent flood, it once again experienced the mighty Missouri coursing over its surface. So, back to U.S. 24 and on to Fort Osage, stopping at several more DAR markers, including the largest on the Trail at Buckner.

As I drove into the parking lot at the Fort visitors center, I was surprised to see several other cars. Apparently, the inclement weather had not deterred a few other people. I dashed into the center, and for the next forty-five minutes toured the tiny museum, browsed through the gift shop, and talked with Joseph Cartwright, assistant museum administrator. Not that all this would normally consume that much time—save for the conversation—but, it was still raining.

Eventually, I drove down to the Fort parking lot and walked quickly to the nearest open building, the factory. Even an umbrella provided only minimal protection against the wind and driving rain. Fort Osage was the guardian of an unexplored frontier from 1808 to 1827. The present structure, like Bent's Old Fort, is a reproduction of the original. We must be reminded that while Fort Osage was a military post, its dual position as a trading post surprisingly eclipsed its policing activities. The Fort civilian administrator, known by the English title "Factor," was the famous George C. Sibley who directed the official survey of the Santa Fe Trail in 1825–1826. He was famous in these parts as well, and the little town on the edge of the Fort bears his name. Mile zero of the survey is here at Fort Osage.

Approaching the factory, I noticed a large Great Pyrenees dog beside the building paddling in the mud. She was chained to a post which also was exposed to the elements. Her normally white coat gave little evidence of the beauty that is this breed, and her paws—oh my, her paws—were huge globs of sticky mud. I was shocked that she was permitted to endure such hardship. Once inside the building I mentioned my concern to the staff person, who was assuming the role of storekeeper. He shook his head and sighed deeply, expressing his frustration that this pup was out in the elements by choice and would not stay on the covered porch or in her dog house when put there. Hopefully, he remarked, when the winter winds and snow make their appearance, Sally will decide that her dog house, with its bed of straw, is not so bad after all. How often other visitors had expressed the same concern I can only surmise.

The name "factory" puzzled me, and I wondered what product the Fort manufactured. Nothing, the storekeeper replied. The term in that day referred to the trade of goods, particularly furs, in which the Fort engaged. Today the store deals mostly in authentically reproduced tinware, primarily dining and cooking utensils for the tourist trade. The stock was fine looking, but the price tag on a coffeepot I admired convinced me that I could do without it.

Reconstruction of the log fort is only about half completed, but since work ceased in the 1960s, the storekeeper was not sure it ever would resume. Jackson County, the current owner, presumably does not have the money.

As we continued to chat and the rain continued to fall, another employee entered. He was garbed in a vintage 1812 infantry uniform. With no visitors for him to guide around the fortress, he came to the factory for some companionship. Since I had not yet seen the remainder of the stronghold, it seemed appropriate that I help relieve his boredom with a tour. He led me to the very crude barracks which was leaking badly, a condition I am sure existed when authentic soldiers were quartered there. The one blockhouse that was open was very sturdily built with finely pointed stone. The structure was spacious, capable of accommodating dozens of men at the gun ports. Even sleeping quarters were available. I mounted the steps to the lookout. This day I was not looking for "unfriendlies" but for a view of the river and beyond. Fog obscured the north bank of the river, but had the day been clear, the view still would have been predominantly water.

My last stop in the Fort complex was the Sibley community cemetery, for the purpose of seeing traces of the grassy ramp the wagons mounted from the river below. A wet walk to the back of the cemetery brought me to the ramp and the DAR marker beside it. The ramp was clearly visible at the brow of the rise, but quickly was enveloped in dense undergrowth as it descended to the riverbank. Today was not the day to go exploring down that slippery slope. Hopefully, I will encounter better weather the next time.

The rain slackened as I left the Fort and soon ceased completely. I stopped at several more DAR markers and then elected to call it a day, choosing to bypass Blue Mills and Independence (originally Wayne City) Landings because of the heavy construction zone I came upon on the east side of Independence. Although industrial development has long since obliterated both landings, and locating the sites may have been fraught with navigational obstacles, I trust I would have succeeded, but probably in the dark. So, I added two more sites to the ever growing list.

In the south section of Kansas City en route to the Silbermans house, my hosts for the next two days, I crossed Indian Creek, which was now a raging, muddy torrent. It was not difficult imagining the problems this small waterway presented to travelers who reached it in springtime—the rainy season. How depressing it must have be to encounter such an obstacle on only the second day out of Independence.

The next day dawned sunny, and it looked like a good day to explore the Trail in metropolitan Kansas City. The Silbermans joined me, as they had on a previous visit. Our route today would begin in Raytown and angle southwest to New Santa Fe, leaving the trailhead at Independence for the following day. Driving through the busy Kansas City streets on a Monday morning looking for Santa Fe Trail sites can best be described as an anachronistic experience, much as was the sight of Shamu, the blimp. It is also an experience that a driver should not undertake alone. A navigator, with guidebook and city map at hand, is a necessity for anyone following the Trail in Kansas City.

We started our tour at the Raytown City Hall, which boasts a bronze plaque of George W. Rhoades at the entrance. Mr. Rhoades was a Jackson County surveyor in the 1840s, but he is of interest to Trail buffs for his advocacy of a public highway to Santa Fe. Other Raytown sites proved not so easy to locate as was this one. However, we did not make too many wrong turns and, amazingly, drove down only one alley and several dead end streets.

When we stopped at the Rice-Tremonti house, the word "anachronistic" popped into my mind again. The house sits among six acres of trees and overgrown shrubs along the busy Blue Ridge Boulevard., a major artery which bisects Kansas City from the Missouri

River on the north to Grandview on the south. The house was built by Farmer Archibald Rice in 1844. As outbound and inbound wagon trains passed his home in an unbroken line from early spring to mid-autumn, he quickly realized he was sitting on a veritable gold mine. So, he commenced selling produce to travelers—the first supermarket on the Santa Fe Trail.

That was not all Entrepreneur Rice had in mind for his food emporium, and as Matt Field described the rest of the operation, "leisure travellers often linger to enjoy his sweet bacon, fresh eggs, new milk, and other nutritious and unsophisticated luxuries...."[5] Could this have been the forerunner to the Harvey House? (Please pardon the use of this oft quoted page, but Field's eloquence cannot be matched by me and apparently others, and thus bears repeating.)

Mel and I walked to the rear of the house, noticing that the weeds were beginning to take possession of the grounds. The house was vacated in 1987 after a hundred forty-three years of continuous occupancy. In 1989 the Friends of the Rice-Tremonti Home Association took a giant leap of faith and bought the house, saddling the Association with a mortgage in excess of a quarter million dollars.

The Friends had completed much restoration by the time of our visit, but as I glanced at the decorative gables, I wondered if integrity was being maintained. A strange protrusion extending above the peak of one such gable did not belong to any period I could identify, but if it did, it appeared out of place and perspective. However, this minor irregularity did not distract from the substantial air the house exuded.

At the far back corner of the property, facing Blue Ridge Boulevard., stood the deteriorating vacant log cabin occupied by Aunt Sophie, a slave of Rice's daughter-in-law, Catherine Stoner White Rice. The fact that the cabin still stands is a marvel in itself. It is no architectural oddity, nor did a famous personage ever occupy it. It stands today, primarily, because it was located in the right place at the right time.

This was Aunt Sophie's home until she died in 1896. Why the one room cabin was not promptly demolished, I do not know. However, when the Missouri chapters of the DAR launched their movement in 1908 to erect Santa Fe Trail markers across the state, "Aunt Sophie's

Kitchen" was a designated location, and the tiny structure assumed a place in history. (The dedication of all state DAR markers occurred May 15, 1913.)

A few blocks farther down Blue Ridge Boulevard. we pulled into Klein Park. The Park's principal point of interest is Cave Spring, the site of a major campground. It holds the distinction of being the only cave on the Trail that also served as a campground. The local Cave Spring Association should be commended for its first-rate preservation and interpretation of the site, which includes an attractive visitors center. The Silbermans elected not to take the nature trail into the woods to the spring because they felt the neighborhood was too dangerous, and with the visitors center closed (of course!), their only option was to sit in the car. I am happy I did not heed their warning, for I would have missed beauty that rivals Lost Spring and Middle Spring. The path descended a gentle hill to a small pond. Just as I approached the pond, a Great Blue Heron spread its huge wings and lifted into the air. I admired his bravery and determination in locating this restful oasis amid the cacophony just beyond these woods. He was migrating south, and I imagined that in a few months I would encounter him again at the Bosque del Apache, a national wildlife refuge in New Mexico.

The path quickly plunged into the woods. Although I was not afraid, it was easy to understand why city born and bred persons who daily encounter human violence would prefer to remain locked in their auto rather than take a short stroll through a secluded woods. I passed the ruins of two stone structures, and assumed that if the visitor center had been open I would have learned more about them. Later, I discovered that these were the remains of seven chimneys from a private country club which occupied the property earlier this century.[6]

Upon taking first one and then a second fork in the main trail, I descended another short hill and found myself at the spring. Not much sunlight filtered through the dense foliage, thus I was not upset that my camera was back at the house. The water appeared to be issuing from the rocky outcropping that formed part of the hill. I returned to the car by way of yet another idyllic trail. No one remarked about my stupidity or bravery, whichever they thought of my hike. In fact, they ignored the entire episode, which I felt was generous of them.

Continuing south, we soon crossed into Kansas City and headed for Lou Schumacher's ruts atop a hill overlooking the city. Although a huge shopping mall was only several blocks away at the base of the hill, the street we were following had a distinctly rural feel, due in no small degree to barns located behind several of the houses. Beside the ruts and a DAR marker was a huge "For Sale" sign. I was taken aback, realizing that less than two years earlier the site had been certified by the NPS. Later, back in Santa Fe, I reread the *Kansas City Star* newspaper articles written about the certification ceremony that occurred November 7, 1991, and discovered that the site being preserved is within a fifty foot wide greenbelt corridor on the south side of the (93rd) street. Knowing that the ruts would be preserved and that a parkway of sorts would surround them was small comfort against the realization that one day this pastoral scene would be shrouded with nondescript buildings much like what the view below took in. I am happy I was able to see it before that occurs. Yet, the ruts have survived urban sprawl, a miracle in itself.

The Fitzhugh-Watts Mill was our next destination, and what a pleasant site it was. Kansas City government has done a splendid job of preserving the space which sits on the banks of picturesque, calm Indian Creek—the very same waterway that had been a fierce and powerful force the previous day. A sizable section of the mill's ground level foundation walls are somewhat protected by sections of post and rail fencing. A fine interpretive marker overlooks the site and the creek beyond. I trust that Mr. John Fitzhugh, who built the mill in 1832, and Mr. Anthony Watts, who bought it in 1850, wherever they are, approve of the city's achievements. Would they also approve of reconstructing the entire mill, which is being considered?

We were now headed for New Santa Fe, our final stop of the day. En route, we detoured slightly to cross the Blue River at Red Bridge Road. This street acquired its name during Trail days when a red bridge was built here. Of course, when the wagons first began rumbling westward there was no bridge at all. Caravans forded the river about three hundred yards north of the present road. The first span, a genuine covered bridge, was built in 1859, thus saw some frontier-bound traffic. Because Minor Park is immediately west of the bridge, we drove by to catch yet another glimpse of those dramatic swales Nogah and I had walked two years before.

New Santa Fe was the last community westbound caravans encountered in Missouri. It was also the junction of the Independence and Westport roads. Today it is nothing more than a typical metropolitan subdivision, complete with the neat but nondescript "ticky-tacky boxes all in a row." The historical marker noting the townsite was located in a cemetery beside a nondescript "ticky-tacky" church. The DAR marker at the corner displayed yet another symptom of modernity—a trench had been dug in front of it by some utility company, bringing yet bigger and better living to this Kansas City outlier.

W.W.H. Davis, en route to Santa Fe in 1853 to assume the office of Secretary of the Territory, had a more memorable time in the little town than did we. This was the second night's stop for the mail-wagon which was carrying Davis to his new post. The passengers were provided accommodations in the mail agent's humble home. But, the crudeness of the structure bespoke little of the cheer within. Davis liberally lauded the culinary skills of the agent's wife. However, he reserved his highest compliment for other talents she displayed, and wrote eloquently of these in his book, *El Gringo: New Mexico and Her People:* "She graced the head of her own table, and, instead of allowing us to eat in moody silence, as hungry men are too apt to do, she maintained a lively conversation.... After supper we drew our chairs around the blazing hearth, and chatted with host and hostess until bedtime."[7] New Santa Fe, thus, provided at least one traveler with an uncommon and memorable beginning to an arduous winter journey.

That evening, reflecting on the day's journey, Nogah and Mel made the time-honored remark I had heard and made often enough myself, "I never knew all this Santa Fe Trail history was here." That is changing, however. Witness the number of newspaper clippings my Kansas friends have sent, and continue to send me, in recent years. The secret of the Trail is no more, and we inveterate Trail buffs must learn to share our special road with others—including bikers.

Note: Four years later (1997) I returned to Missouri to see what the flood waters had denied me on that first trip. My first stop was at Rivercene, where I would spend two nights with Jody and Ron

Lenz. Recalling my first glimpse of the flood-ravaged mansion, I apprehensively drove down the road wondering the nature of the sight my eyes would behold. At the circular driveway I stopped, alighted from my car and gazed in unabashed joy and wonder at the regal sight before me. Rivercene had undergone a transformation, presenting an appearance that would have been familiar to Captain Kinney. But something was missing—the stately trees (regrettably, I never learned their species) that shaded the drive from road to doorstep. Sadly, they had not survived the flood.

Jody greeted me at the door, and after I had settled in she gave me the grand tour, filling in the details of their restoration efforts following my 1993 visit. The transformation was miraculous, and the wood trim throughout gleamed even brighter after as many as seven cleanings in some areas. That evening, still talking "clean-up," Ron showed me nineteenth century photos of the house and grounds. In one, a riverboat was docked just at the edge of the present road that fronts the house. Now the road is several miles north of the water's edge, confirming that Old Muddy's meanderings never cease.

The next morning I went to the Old Franklin site. New Markers had been erected, replacing those that disappeared somewhere in those torrential waters. Maybe they have found their way to New Orleans. The site was neat and somewhat antiseptic in looks—not my concept of what the hundred seventy-five-year-old trailhead should be.

On to historic Arrow Rock, where my hosts were SFTA founders Ginny and Ted Fisher. I was introduced to Adam, the proud and pompous peacock, and Merry Christmas, the "senior" Sheltie, both who are the true lords of that household. I wanted to see the Arrow Rock landing where the caravans crossed the Missouri River from Old Franklin. Ted said we would try, but as we tromped through the waist-high underbrush, I could appreciate the verb. Every few minutes he would warn me of the poison ivy snaking about in all directions, not that the warning was necessary, for I have done battle with that vine before and lost miserably. It was quickly apparent that June was no time to locate any ruts that still might exist, so we retraced our steps. Ginny had arranged a visit to Ed Weinreich's celebrated ruts near Marshall. But first, lunch, a most refreshing culinary salad direct from the Fishers garden topped off with home-baked bread, served al fresco on their tree-surrounded deck.

Ed met us at his house, and we piled into his pickup and bumped along his pasture into a moderately dense woods. En route he gave us a bit of history of the farm, which had been in his family for a hundred and nineteen years. When a St. Louis cemetery where some of his ancestors were buried informed him the cemetery was being moved, he bought the family gravestones and moved them to his front yard. Sure enough, they were there. Another of his talents was being declared the 1959 automatic corn picker national champion. Ed's ruts, although not as thick as that at the Arrow Rock landing, still were hard to define. The best perspective appeared with Ed standing in the ruts and Ted atop the edge, some five feet above. So, I took several pictures.

For Trail travelers who roam about the Rocky Mountains or the Kansas high plains, the "jungles" of Missouri may seem arduous to navigate, and the route hard to locate. In many places it would appear the most useful tool in the freighters arsenal would have been a machete. (Did Dr. Sappington have a remedy for poison ivy?) Back in the pickup, we again bounced along to a pasture where Ed pointed out the route of the Trail back toward Arrow Rock. Four gigantic Charolais bulls were lounging around with nothing better to do than stare at us and chew their cud. A bit uneasy—the largest weighed twenty-four hundred pounds—I cautiously walked beside Ed, opposite those bulls, with my eyes steadily trained on the nearby truck in case a quick retreat was required. The bulls are cream puffs, he chuckled. The largest expects a back rub every morning.

As always, goodbyes along the Trail are pensive, and it was no different when I left Ginny and Ted, heading for Independence. I revisited a number of sites, and stopped at Tabo Creek which had been inaccessible in 1993 due to the flood. Across the highway just east of the creek I noted Ginny's ancestral home, Old Oaks. The years have been kind to it, and its present occupants have cared for it well.

On this day the fishermen were out and lining the creek's banks. Evidence of recent partying was strewn about, the latter most assuredly bearing no resemblance to the dance pavilion and camping ground across the creek which graced the area and attracted the locals—young and old alike—in the 1930s.

Walking down the somewhat steep descent to the water's edge where in Trail days a ferry waited to transport the wagons across the creek, this appeared to me to be a tricky crossing, even accounting for normal ground-shifting. With the May 1991 issue of *Wagon Tracks* in hand, I sat on a rock and read Ginny Fisher's informative article about Tabo Creek.[8] Not only is Ginny a knowledgeable historian, but she writes with a wry sense of humor.

Next was Lexington, another treasure the rain forced me to abandon on my earlier excursion. First, I drove through the historic district to view the many antebellum houses, a hundred nineteen which are listed on the National Register of Historic Places, for which the town is known. These included several Trail freighters and merchants. Then to the Civil War Battle of Lexington site, now a lovely green park set high above the Missouri River. The walking path around the site was well marked with signs interpreting the September 18-20, 1861 battle. Interestingly, this was known as the "Battle of the Hemp Bales," signifying the barricades behind which the Confederate troops crouched.

Moving along, I was eager to see Fort Osage in dry sunlight instead of the unrelenting rain I encountered four years earlier. This time I strolled more leisurely around the grounds, reading each interpretive marker. I stopped by the factor's store to say hello to Sally, the Great Pyrenees, only to discover she had taken up residence at a nearby farm. As before, I visited the Sibley cemetery before leaving the area. At the DAR marker at the crest of the ramp to the Missouri River, I came upon a family from Kansas City on a Sunday historical excursion. A lady was describing the site and its historical significance in some detail. I noticed she was carrying Simmons' Trail guide. We began chatting, and I learned she was a school teacher who included a western trails unit in her Missouri history curriculum. I suggested she consider adding Dave Webb's *Adventures with the Santa Fe Trail* activity book.

Independence: after a full day it was a joy to pull up in front of what was to be my home for the next two days, Serendipity, an elegant nineteenth century Victorian home turned bed and breakfast, three blocks south of Independence Square. Entering into the spacious foyer, I was greeted by tinkling music from a music box, a sound that would be ever-present during my stay. Susan Walter, the B&B owner, gave me a tour through all the house, which was replete with antique furniture, colored and cut glass, porcelain figurines, but most prominent were dolls and more dolls seated and reclining wherever a comfortable space could be found. Susan escorted me to my "Garden Room," i.e., basement. Well, I did have privacy, and the bed was comfy.

My guides next day—a day fuller than last—were SFTA luminaries Jane Mallinson and Polly Fowler, plus Eric, Polly's son. First, we made a quick run to Blue Mills and Wayne City Landings, where in Trail days merchandise was off-loaded from river boats and packed in Santa Fe-bound wagons. Jane was involved in developing the latter overlook which featured fine interpretive markers. A steep hill rose from the Missouri River to Independence Square. Mule power was employed to haul the cargo to town, and would you believe, these valiant animals rode on a wagon back down the hill to pick up another load. Pretty cushy, right?

Next was Woodlawn Cemetery where we engaged in a scavenger hunt searching for the resting places of celebrated Santa Fe Trail persons. We each headed in a different direction and walked a section, waving our arms when the "hunt" succeeded. Graves we found included: Hiram Young (wagonmaker), John Lewis (freighter), Emily Fisher (ex-slave, entrepreneur), Smallwood Noland (hotel proprietor), William and John McCoy (merchants), and, not least, Mother Matilda Mills, appointed as superior of Sisters of Loretto ,who died of cholera, that dread disease, the name alone which put fear in men's hearts, aboard a steamer between St. Louis and Independence, en route to Santa Fe.[9]

Not to be outdone by Lexington, Independence has its own collection of classical nineteenth century homes. The Lewis-Webb house was our first stop, and I knew we were in for a treat. The tidy two-story brick house with gingerbread latticework trim on the expansive porch and dormers was built by John Lewis, a Trail trader, saddlemaker, and builder. We gazed over the picket fence to find two dogs, four or five turkeys, a guinea fowl, and more, all getting along just fine. A young lady emerged from the house, and thus we met Dawn Coary, who has been interested in the Trail but because of all the demands on restoring her home has not become involved in SFTA. Jane and Polly have some work to do. Independence's first mayor, William McCoy and also a Trail trader, built his elegant brick home in 1856, our next stop. Moving on, Smallwood Noland, proprietor of the Noland House hotel where Susan Magoffin spent the night before starting her epic journey westward, built a stately mansion south of the public square. It is situated on broad acreage, which is surprising being in the center of a vast urban area. Huge trees surrounded the house, making it difficult to see the full extent of the house's elegance, and totally impossible to photograph well. On we cruised, pausing at more architectural gems.

Lastly were the ruts in Santa Fe Trail Park, and even better ones just beyond. Eric knocked on the door at 3101 S. Santa Fe Road, and was dumbfounded to see a former high school girl friend on the other side. We walked to the side yard where excellent ruts ran under a swing and down a gentle slope to a field beyond. Daylight was waning, so after bidding Jane and Eric a heartwarming thanks and farewell, Polly and I wrapped up that perfect day with dinner.

Lou Schumacher joined me for a tasty and bountiful breakfast the next morning, testing Susan's numerous talents, with the tinkling music box melodies hovering around us. We headed south to 85th and Manchester streets where we saw stunning ruts coursing diagonally across a good-sized corner lot, probably the only vacant lot within miles. But this was not the site Lou was aiming for. We headed up a hill, and here was yet another vacant lot—Schumacher Park—Lou's property, which he has preserved for the Trail. The site commands an excellent view of south Kansas City. Fine ruts run through it, with an attractive kiosk to one side containing panels interpreting the Trail's history through this part of the city. Lou had recently planted wildflower and native grasses seed, and was eager to see the fruits of his labor. A huge Bullmastiff followed us as we toured the garden. I am sure he was hanging on Lou's every word, learning much about the Santa Fe Trail. It was time to reluctantly bid Lou goodbye, and thank him for a fantastic day.

There was just enough time to drive by William Bent's little cottage, and perhaps this time someone would be around to allow me a closer look. This was Bent's home away from home, where he stopped on his numerous eastern business trips, and where his young daughters, Julia and Mary, lived while allegedly in school. However, David Lavender could find no record of Julia's education.[10] Amazingly, a lady was in the side yard tending her garden with the able assistance of a St. Bernard "pup" (can a two hundred forty pound dog truly be defined as a "pup"?) named Orion (a fitting name for a dog equal to the size of its namesake heavenly constellation), and three or four black Newfoundlands. The "Newfees" literally looked like pups beside Orion. Now, "Newfees" are no small dogs, their average weight being a hundred ten to a hundred fifty pounds. Imagine having eight hundred-plus pounds of house dogs constantly underfoot. With so much overly enthusiastic dog scampering about, it was considered unwise for me to enter the yard for a close view of the Bent house, so again I was denied close inspection. Dare I hope, next time?

As I write, I must admit that the numerous trips I have made along the Trail are beginning to blur together. It is not possible to remember how many times I have visited a particular site, and what were the years. Thus, when I visited the Grinter house and ferry crossing I cannot say, yet the house inside and out and the expansive lawn are blazoned indelibly in my mind for all time. Moses Grinter began operating his ferry on the Kaw River in January, 1831. Located on the north bank of the river on the west boundary of present Kansas City, Kansas, it served the California and Oregon emigrants, and was the main military road south from Fort Leavenworth to Fort Gibson, Oklahoma, and as a feeder route to the Santa Fe Trail during the Mexican- American War. Grinter built his stately brick house in 1857 on a high hill commanding a stunning view of the river where the ferry cruised, and the prairie opposite. Of all the fine homes I have seen perched atop a hill, in my view, this is the most breathtaking. Thus, there is no better place to end this chapter than beside this majestic house on a green hill overlooking the ferry landing aimed toward Santa Fe.

Notes

1. Davis, H. Denny. Franklin: Cradle of the Trade. *Wagon Tracks,* 1993, 7(3), pgs. 11-17.

2. Strate, David K. (Ed.). *West by Southwest: Letters of Joseph Pratt Allyn, A Traveller Along the Santa Fe Trail, 1863.* Dodge City, Kansas: Heritage Center, 1984.

3. Maier, M.A. Pecan Time. *New Mexico,* November, 1993.

4. Garrard, Lewis. *Wah-to-yah and the Taos Trail.* Norman, Oklahoma: University of Oklahoma Press, 1955, p. 39.

5. Sunder, John E. (Ed.). *Matt Field on the Santa Fe Trail.* Norman, Oklahoma: University of Oklahoma Press, 1960, p. 70.

6. Mooney, Sylvia D. Cave Spring: Historic Landmark on the Santa Fe Trail. *Wagon Tracks,* 1988, 3(1), p. 7.

7. Davis, W.W.H. El Gringo: New Mexico and Her People. Lincoln, Nebraska: University of Nebraska Press, 1982, p. 16.

8. Fisher, Virginia. Tabo Creek. *Wagon Tracks,* 1991, 5(3), pgs. 8-9.

9. Cook, Mary J. Straw. *Loretto: The Sisters and Their Chapel.* Santa Fe, New Mexico: Museum of New Mexico Press, 2002, pgs. 9-10.

10. Lavender, David. *Bent's Fort.* Lincoln, Nebraska: University of Nebraska Press, 1954, p. 445, n.8.

Grand Pass Cemetery, Grand Pass, Missouri.

Fort Osage near Kansas City, Missouri.

Ed Weinreich ruts Marshall, Missouri.

Woodlawn Cemetery, Independence, Missouri.

7

Harry's Independence

The day following our 1993 (Kansas City) Raytown excursion was reserved for Independence (see chapter 6, "Floating Across Missouri"). Even during the planning process it was obvious that historical Independence cannot be seen in a day, previous visits notwithstanding. Again, my friends and hosts, the Silbermans, would join me. Our tour started at Independence Square where so many wagon trains of yore also began their westward journey. Instead of droves of oxen, mules, and covered wagons, we were faced with hordes of automobiles and trucks.

The Jackson County Courthouse forms the centerpiece of the Square. The present structure is quite large by American courthouse standards, and antedates the Trail. However, some foundation sections do date back to the earlier structure which did exist when Independence, founded in 1827, was literally the Queen City of the Western Trails. Architecturally handsome though the present building is, I was seeking a more rugged, frontier ambiance which could propel me a hundred fifty years and more back in time. That was to come from the writings of persons who lived the experience rather than many of the buildings in the town.

Susan Magoffin spent several days in Independence prior to her journey, shopping and exchanging visits with local friends. She and trader husband Sam stayed at the stately Noland House, the largest and most comfortable hotel west of St. Louis. It was located one block north of Courthouse Square, and Simmons claims that the building standing there today has incorporated some of the original structure within its walls.

Matt Field's description of the start of a caravan's journey paints a mental picture that is unmatched. He wrote the following for the New Orleans *Picayune* newspaper:

> In the square you observe a number of enormous wagons into which men are packing bales and boxes. Presently the mules are driven in from pasture, and a busy time commences..., catching the fractious animals.... Full half a day is thus employed before the expedition finally gets into motion and winds slowly out of town. This is an exciting moment. Every window sash is raised [as the townsfolk watch] the departure... Accidents are very apt to occur on the occasion of a setting out.... [O]n the day of our departure [a] drunken driver lashed his mules into a fright and then tumbled into the road, while the team dashed aside, and dragged the loaded vehicle down a steep lane over stumps and stones and other inequalities with most dangerous velocity, until they were brought up against a log house in the middle of the way.[1]

Ah, yes, these essays from the past put Independence into the perspective I was seeking. However, the 1993 version of the town holds much for the history buff, not the least which is a magnificent bronze statue of a jauntily strolling Harry S. Truman, with cane in hand and hat on head. Not even the seated Lincoln on the Mall in Washington, DC is more moving to me, politics aside.

We toured every building near the square that related to the Trail, and while it was a bit early for lunch, decided that we could find no better eatery than the old fashioned Clinton Drugstore across from the Courthouse. It was here that Harry Truman secured his first paying job. The drugstore had an authentic soda fountain and a tiny dining area furnished with authentic wire framed tables and chairs. The crowning glory to all this nostalgia was a genuine chocolate soda in a genuine soda glass. Could anything in life be more satisfying?

After that tasty treat we drove down Liberty, the street the wagon trains took as they left the square and, no doubt, the one Matt Field described in the quotation above, past the site of Robert Weston's blacksmith shop. It stands to reason that old Bob was heavily involved in the western trails. Then on to the Kritser house, built by Martin L. Kritser from profits earned in the Santa Fe trade. The small house built of brick surprised me. Although brick was not an unknown commodity in 1847 when the house was built, it was somewhat a luxury. The house held interest for me in another way, for Martin was the great-grandfather of Dave Masterman, a Santa Fe Trail authority who resides in Santa Fe.

Martin Kritser made a single trip across the Trail, I learned from Dave, and that was in the year 1846. He was among the huge flock of traders who followed Brig. General Stephen Kearny's Army of the West en route to the southwest to kick off the Mexican-American War. Kritser braved the vicious winter on the prairie to return home, arriving in Independence in February of 1847. His caravan met not a single soul during the eastward crossing.

The windows and doors of the house were boarded up, but otherwise it appeared in fairly good condition. How long the little house will be able to withstand the encroachment of commercialization coming at it from all directions remains to be seen. Possibly even more hazardous is the vibration against those fragile walls from a constant stream of traffic along the major thoroughfare at its doorstep.

Our next stop was the elegant Bingham-Waggoner estate, a twenty-six room Victorian mansion set amid nineteen wooded acres along the trails to the west. It was built in 1855 by John Lewis, a saddle-maker, who, like so many other residents of Independence, made his living from the Santa Fe trade. For the first year of its life the house silently watched the huge caravans slowly move past on their way out of town. But, in 1856 the trailhead moved west, and the house was left with memories only. Not entirely, however, for during the Civil War it witnessed two battles fought directly in its front yard.

Touring this elegant, yet homey mansion could not be rushed, and we did not. The hand-painted linen wallpaper gracing many of the rooms and the mahogany woodwork in the dining room were especially striking. Outside, a spacious wrap-around porch called up visions of large soirees as well as intimate family gatherings at the end of the day. It also provided a dangerously intimate viewing platform for those Civil War battles.

Already the day was quickly ebbing, so we were forced to make a very hurried turn through the recently National Park Service certified National Frontier Trails Center. However, some things cannot be overlooked, which at the museum included the Santa Fe Trail exhibit and a very fine interpretive film. As we rushed to the parking lot after viewing the collection, ominous clouds had gathered—tornado weather, for sure.

The Valle mansion was our next destination, and the final tour of the day was beginning just as we hurried up the front steps. This outstanding Second Empire style 31-room three-story mansion, said to be one of the finest examples of Victorian architecture in the entire country, was built by Harvey Merrick Valle in 1881. Although the house does not come within the Trail period, its builder does. In 1870 Colonel Valle bought the Star Mail Route which carried mail throughout the west, including along the Santa Fe Trail. From the looks of this stately mansion, the overland mail business must have been quite profitable for the Colonel. Too much so, thought the federal government whom he was accused of defrauding. Fortunately for Valle, he was acquitted of all charges. Each room produced more "oohs" and "ahs" from us than the last, and by the time the tour was completed, we felt that both the Valle and Bingham-Waggoner estate had shown us the finest possible examples of nineteenth century elegant living.

Note: Both of these houses are decorated each Christmas season, and touring them is a holiday highlight for many Kansas Citizens. The Silbermans went on the tour, and Nogah reported as follows: "Decorations at the Valle were spectacular: Never have I seen such opulence and yet done so artfully. Cannot rave enough.... The B-W house...was not coordinated, nor very attractive. But the house speaks for itself." Indeed, the house *does* speak for itself.

Thus ended—quite abruptly, I might add—this tour of the easternmost section of the Trail. Several tornadoes did touch down in the greater metropolitan area, but fortunately, not in the Silbermans neighborhood. No major damage occurred to humans or structures anywhere in Kansas City that day. Nor were any wagon train departures delayed.

As packed as each day had been, I still had missed a great deal of this end of the Trail, and it was obvious that a return visit must be scheduled in the near future. Tomorrow I would head for Kansas where I planned to stop at several sites previously bypassed unintentionally and revisit a few old favorites.

Notes

1. Sunder, John E. (Ed.). *Matt Field on the Santa Fe Trail*. Norman, Oklahoma: University of Oklahoma Press, 1960, pgs. 64-65.

8

Cruising Around New Mexico

Jaunts to Trail sites in New Mexico often are single day excursions, similar to that first drive to La Cueva (see Introduction). Most I have visited more than once, each time finding something that had previously escaped my attention.

Las Vegas is a good example. Two excellent swales intersect I-25, aiming toward the Old Town Plaza. I had to drive the two-plus mile stretch between exits several times before traffic conditions allowed me to look for them at the right place. It was certainly worth the effort to see these scooped out grassy depressions.

Why, or perhaps how, I missed the Jose Albino Baca house, located in the Upper Plaza area on the north side of town, during my first tour I do not know, particularly since before- and after-remodeling photos appear in Simmons' guide. Perhaps it was because the integrity has been severely compromised by the remodeling, and I did not recognize that, indeed, this was the house for which I was searching. Baca was a successful trader and prominent Las Vegas citizen who built this fine three-story house in the 1850s.

The most famous building on the Old (Lower) Plaza still standing from Trail days is an adobe structure from whose flat roof Brig. General Stephen Kearny proclaimed on August 15, 1846 that New Mexico was now a territory of the U.S. Of course, this happened during the Mexican-American War. (Was that one of the "wars to end all wars?") Old Plaza is the current center of town, the site of most special events.

New Mexico Highlands University campus, a short distance across the Gallinas River from Old Plaza, contains two fine campgrounds utilized during the Trail days. Both have been spared development, although university buildings do surround these grassy greens. One of the campgounds, located several blocks north of the Trail—now named National Avenue—was a popular overnight stop for wagon trains. The other, fronting National Avenue, was the spot General Kearny selected to bivouac his troops before marching to the Plaza to deliver that speech from atop that adobe building.

Kearny's campground at National Avenue is situated on a prominent rise overlooking the Plaza. The view on this spot extends to the foothills beyond town, almost to the next important Trail site to the southwest—Kearny Gap. I wonder if the soldiers took the time to take in this splendid sight. All this and more I learned when the End of the Trail chapter was treated to a walking tour of the Old Plaza area by Michael Olsen, Highlands professor and Santa Fe Trail authority.

Kearny Gap is a natural pass the Trail followed, which was the route the General's army took heading for Santa Fe after he climbed down from that roof. Each time I visit this stunning geological formation I learn and see something new. For example, with the help of binoculars I can now see in great detail the ruins of a stage station which is in the middle of an overgrown field. Fine ruts lead from the Gap, pass the ruins, and fan out in a southerly direction. Unfortunately, all are behind a forbidding barbed wire fence.

The most informative visit to this site was a field trip organized by the Corazon de los Caminos chapter of the Santa Fe Trail Association at which Harry Myers, Superintendent of Fort Union, recounted his research of the historic and most surprising meeting between Captain Pedro Ignacio Gallego and William Becknell in 1821. Harry and Mike Olsen—the Bobsey twins of the Santa Fe Trail—made this startling discovery when Gallego's previously unknown diary was unearthed in the New Mexico state archives. This was Becknell's first journey to Santa Fe, but he became hopelessly lost until he came upon the Captain and some four hundred Mexican soldiers who courteously pointed the tiny troop in the right direction.

Possibly, it was on this field trip that I learned who owned the property which contained a stage station and those magnificent ruts. "Wink" Winkel is his name. I met him at a Corazon de los Caminos field trip to his historic place. He was most eager to set an appointment when I could return and get behind that fence. When I did return, I was not disappointed. The stage station ruins were most dramatic, as I usually find dilapidating structures. "Wink's" dogs joined Lance, my current canine companion, and me on our tour of the ruins and ruts. The ruts have been significantly eroded to approximately twelve feet below ground level, somewhat similar to the Durham Blowout in Kansas. How fortunate that "Wink" is a SFTA member, and has generously opened his gems to others.

A little farther south the ruts, which at this point are paralleled by a housing development road, have been severely eroded. These are not as dramatic as the Kansas "Durham Blowout," but hold a close second. Because they are not behind fences, Demi and I have walked these ruts several times. On the opposite side of the road are yet more ruts, which gradually mount a gentle rise into a piñon and juniper forest.

At the south terminus of the road, the Trail turned west and passed through yet another and even more dramatic gap, the Puertocito Pedregosa—little rocky gate, in Spanish—whose gnarled and jagged stone walls emit a multicolored glow. Beyond the gate a gravel road winds around the escarpment and enters a tiny ribbon of level ground upon which are imprinted the finest yet traces of the Trail in this overpowering region. The ruts have eroded slightly, creating brick red earthen banks which clearly define the route the wagons followed. This is a favorite spot of mine, and whenever I am in the area and time permits, I swing off the interstate for another view. Would that the view was not restricted to the roadside by a heavily padlocked gate.

The next stop for the westbound caravans was Tecolote, meaning owl in Spanish. The little town bears a striking resemblance to many other northern New Mexico villages—a few houses and farm structures gathered around an adobe mission church. The whitewashed church was built in 1846, and continues to serve an active congregation. It was in Tecolote that Marion and Richard Russell opened a trading post after Richard was mustered out of the U.S. Army in 1866. Their store stood on the opposite side of the plaza from the church. But, it exists no longer except in the celestial memories of its famous occupants. I wonder if the angel Marion now strolls the dusty plaza, peering out beyond the last house for a glimpse of a ghostly caravan slowly descending a distant rise.

Continuing down the Trail, fine ruts exist along the frontage road between Bernal and San Miguel del Vado, although there is question whether these are the Trail or remnants of a local road. Yet, I must confess that ruts of any ancient road fascinate me because of their durability, their ability to capture my imagination, and the stories they tell.

A stroll through San Miguel is nothing less than a journey back in time. Remove the few autos and utility poles, and I am sure William Becknell would have no difficulty recognizing it as the village to which Captain Gallego directed him after their historic meeting back at Kearny Gap in 1821.

In 1993 the End of the Trail chapter toured the village. Our guide was Alicia Bustamante, owner of the original customs house. As prelude, Marc Simmons presented an eloquent historic sketch of the village at the ford of the Pecos River. The tour began at the lovely white stucco mission church that was built between 1805 and 1811, and has changed not all that much in the almost two centuries since. This was only the second time in all of my visits to San Miguel that the church doors were open and I was granted the privilege to be in the sanctuary, which was predominantly white with gilt trim.

Alicia then led us on a spritely tour of the village, starting at the supposed Customs House, which she is presently restoring. The authenticity of both the Customs House and the restoration are in question, waiting on funds to conduct the necessary archaeological and historical research.

The Trail forded the Pecos River at the east edge of town, although no trace of its exact location has yet been located. But on that day sixty instant archaeological "experts" claimed they found it. Of course, even they could not agree among themselves on its precise location.

How often I have visited Pecos National Historic Park (13 miles farther west), the centerpiece being the remnants of a pueblo village and Spanish mission church and convento, escapes me. However, only on several occasions was the Trail my goal. The first time, I asked the superintendent for directions. She pointed me in the general direction, but it was so general that the only tracks I located were a National Park Service road. The second and third visits were only a little more fruitful even though they were arranged tours for the End of the Trail chapter. Those experiences plus others convinced me that the park staff were either ignorant of the Santa Fe Trail history or held a negative attitude toward our chapter. Sadly, evidence of the latter did exist.

The third tour focused exclusively on Kozlowski's ranch and stage station and trace remnants nearby. This was a major stage stop, and Mrs. Kozlowski's cooking expertise was applauded up and down the western end of the Trail. Eveline Alexander, wife of a Fort Union cavalry officer, noted in her diary that she was treated to a "delightful supper and breakfast consisting of trout, broiled turkey, omelette, potatoes, etc."[1]

The ranch gained further notoriety as Union Army headquarters during the Civil War Battle of Glorieta Pass. A nearby spring was the primary reason Kozlowski chose this location for his enterprise. Unfortunately, we had to be content with viewing it from some distance and behind a fence. Hopefully, the NPS will soon improve this newly acquired property so that future field trips will be possible to the spring, campground, and ruts, all which are presently closed to the public and Santa Fe Trail Association chapters. Fine ruts supposedly exist in front of the church ruins, but they were not included in the tour either. Quite candidly, most End of the Trail members on that tour are more knowledgeable about the Trail than was our guide.

Reading Susan Magoffin's description of her visit to Pecos pueblo, I am moved by her sensitivity. She wrote, "It created sad thoughts when I found myself riding almost heedlessly over the work of these once mighty people. There perhaps was pride, power and wealth, carried to its utter most limit...."[2]

My initial introduction to the "End of the Trail" chapter occurred a few miles down the road at the Glorieta battlefield, often dubbed the "Gettysburg of the West." Don E. Alberts, who is an eminent authority on the battle, guided us across the rugged terrain. It was on this field trip I learned that the Trail is directly beneath the highway (New Mexico 50), and that if the asphalt were removed, undisturbed ruts would be found, in all likelihood. That is most astounding and puzzling.

A short distance west of the battlefield the final pull into Santa Fe climbed up a canyon onto what is locally called Apache Ridge. In 1859 the U.S. Army constructed stone earthworks along the stretch to stabilize it, distinct remains which still may be seen. This is another special site I visit frequently, and each time I am treated to a memorable experience. In July 1993 I organized an End of the Trail field trip down the canyon, and even today I can hear the exclamations of the group as we traversed this extremely rocky trace. Whether it was the beauty or the sheer treacherousness of the road, these modern day trailers were in awe. How ever did those wagons make it up this boulder strewn defile?

Experiencing the Trail in Santa Fe can occur under the most ordinary of circumstances. For example, I will stop by any number of ruts while running errands. Returning from the Santa Fe ski basin, I sometimes stop at the Fort Marcy site. The Fort, erected in 1846–1847 during the Mexican-American War, was located on a promontory roughly a mile north of the Plaza, and commanded a fine view of the city. It was never occupied, the soldiers being billeted in quarters directly off the Plaza. The fortress crumbled to the ground long ago, and today only low earthen mounds reveal its basic outline.

As a child, Marion Russell played in the Fort's ruins. On a visit to Santa Fe in her later years she strolled the Fort pointing out specific areas her memories called up. She recalled, "Some bleached old bones [from the military burying ground] were lying there.... [W]e gathered [them] up...and played a game we called, 'Steal the Dead Man's Bones.' When our parents found it out the bones were taken from us. 'Tis a fantastic thing to remember."[3]

Today, as since Santa Fe's beginnings, the life of the community centers around the Plaza and the Palace of Governors. The Palace was built in 1610 and, although smaller today, it looks much as it did then and when freighters, over two centuries later, drove their wagons onto the Plaza which the Palace faces. Today, Native Americans sell their arts under the Palace portal, this being not so different from the manner in which the traders sold from their wagons. But, the dust and mud that was the Plaza has now been replaced with grass and park benches.

Demi enjoyed strolling on the cool shaded lawn of the Federal Building, two blocks north of the Plaza, before which stands a monument to Kit Carson. We always took a turn around it before leaving. Moving on, the grave of Charles Bent is located in the Santa Fe National Cemetery, a half dozen blocks north of the Plaza. We have paid our respects in snow, rain, and sunshine.

For a time I frequently stopped at a vacant lot in an up-scale neighborhood on the south side of the city where the Trail descends from the mountains heading for the Plaza. Two sets of ruts in pristine condition intersected the lot from front to back. I wanted that property, and for a brief time even considered paying the $120,000 asking price. However, I did not, and now a nondescript house sits right in the middle, and the ruts are no more. This all happened after I had asked the builder to call me when development appeared imminent. Of course, I never heard from him. Frenetic development is threatening ruts throughout the city, and I anxiously wonder if within not too many years any evidence of that noble road will remain at the end of the Trail.

Eventually in my travels I returned to the Cimarron area when the Old Aztec Mill Museum, Villa Philmonte, and the Kit Carson house were open. The four spacious floors of the Mill were jammed with nineteenth century relics, including a small Santa Fe Trail exhibit. But, it was the substantial stone structure itself that was the centerpiece of the exhibits. At Villa Philmonte I joined a large group of scouts to tour this handsome mansion. This did not match the private showing I received on my first visit, but I learned more about the Villa on this tour, and the opportunity to be within its walls again was appreciated.

Kit Carson's museum at Rayado is built around an interior placita, but what small portion of the adobe structure is the original was not known by the scouts who staffed the facility. The exhibit essentially is a simply furnished house and out-buildings depicting the late 1840s when Kit lived here. Aside from parents visiting their scout sons at the Philmont Boy Scout Ranch, it is doubtful many people know about or visit the museum. It is a certainty that even fewer have seen the Trail ruts round about it.

While these ruts are fine looking, the original road was something else. Major John C. McFerran reported in his military journal of 1864 that the road was in wretched condition from Ocate crossing, twenty-two miles south of Rayado, north to several miles east of Cimarron.[4]

Back on US 64 east of Cimarron I stopped at Colfax, now a ghost town because it could not survive in this sparsely populated area. What remained of the town, which post-dates the Trail, was behind a fence, so I was compelled to view the ruins from a distance. Backtracking to a secondary highway that would take me to I-25, I caught a view of the Wagon Mound from an angle and distance that was new to me. Although caravans following the Mountain Route did not pass this famous landmark, their eyes must have been focused on this distant view of it for ever so long as were mine. I wondered what their thoughts were.

An hour later I was standing at the base of Wagon Mound myself. I had come here to see if this time the gates to Santa Clara Cemetery were open so I could locate the grave site of Charles Fraker, a Trail freighter. Indeed, they were open, and in a short time I located the handsome white marble monument with its exquisite carving of an oxen-drawn covered wagon. Sadly, vandals have defaced it, but not to the point of rendering it unrecognizable.

Not so fortunate was I in reaching Santa Clara Spring, source of water and a fine resting place for caravans. It is on private land, and the owner is not sympathetic to Trail enthusiasts who wish to visit it. Of course, had I been an employee of the NPS, no barrier would have been placed before me. On the positive side, perhaps NPS personnel will be able to persuade the owner to change his mind.

By the time I again cruised onto the interstate, twilight was upon the land. The shadows being cast upon the exquisite ruts I came upon a few miles down the road heading for Santa Fe presented them in excellent relief. It is true that every time one views ruts Mother Nature displays a different cloak, and at twilight she is adorned in her finest.

A few years later, when my knowledge of the Trail and its authorities had expanded, I learned that the Spring may not have been visited by wagon trains because Wagon Mound, several miles south where the Trail actually existed, has an abundant water supply. In 2000 the Spring area was the location of another excellent Corazon event, a barbeque hosted by the owner of the ranch, Harold Daniels. We drove through a bison herd, explored corral ruins, viewed the Spring, and strolled among several possible grave sites, although New Mexico state archaeologists cannot confirm the latter.

On an unusually balmy day in January 1994 I invited a friend, Joan Sudborough, to "hit the Trail" with me and Demi. Our immediate destination was the ghost town, Loma Parda, located six miles southwest of Fort Union. Loma Parda held the dubious distinction of being the wildest town in New Mexico territory, its primary customers being the soldiers from the Fort. Numerous stories have abounded relating to its colorful history, but I am content to fantasize about black haired Mexican ladies bedecked in white ruffly off-the-shoulder blouses and many-colored tiered peasant skirts supported by full petticoats, and a croupier with green eyeshade, red sleeve garters, and a long cigar propped in the corner of his mouth.

The town ruins were on the floor of a canyon along the banks of the Mora River. As we rounded the last curve in the road, sections of walls rose from the ground across the river. Only a footbridge provided access to the town and the occupied house in front. Four very noisy dogs announced our arrival. They gathered around Demi, who ignored them as only a Bulldog can. Her age had precluded walks of any distance, so we left her in the car and crossed the rickety bridge. Once across, we could see the remains of many more buildings. At its zenith, Loma Parda boasted more than one hundred buildings and four hundred residents.

The first ruin, a hotel, was quite spectacular, with one second story section towering over all. Most of the buildings were constructed of red stone which had been quarried or picked up at the site. From the amount of stone still scattered about, several more Loma Pardas easily could have been built. The stone used varied in size from thin flagstone to massive boulders. We walked around the buildings, gazing through several windows and doors which still stood. At the eastern edge of town I located two sets of quite distinct ruts, one heading northeast over a piñon and juniper forested ridge and the other eastward. I decided the left route through the piñon/juniper forest was the road to Fort Union.

Having spent a leisure hour or more strolling around town, we headed back to the bridge and the boisterous dogs who were waiting for us. As we passed the house, a man emerged. We explained our mission and asked about the local history. His ancestors came to the area from Las Vegas in the 1830s and were probably among the founding settlers. The ruts climbing the right side, not those circling the left side of the ridge, led to the Fort. Hmmm, I wonder. When I asked what he thought of the ruins, "pretty neat" was his reply. With a parting look at the ruins we thanked him for allowing us to visit this impressive site, crossed the bridge—which appeared to sway more on our exiting than entering—and drove up out of the canyon.

En route back to I-25 we stopped at the Sapello Stage Station. A New Mexico state historic plaque was attached to the wall of the long, restored building. Although I have never seen evidence of occupation, it reputedly is an inhabited private residence. Several sets of fine ruts sit on high ground paralleling the dirt road opposite the station. This is the Mountain Route. The ruts cross the road shortly past the station and dip down to the shady bank of Sapello Creek where they meet the Cimarron Cutoff. This is yet another splendid site (or is it "sight?") along the Trail.

A short distance beyond the station the road ends at a fine stone corral which presently serves as a rodeo grounds. It was built by William Krönig, a local rancher and farmer, probably in the 1860s. Krönig held contracts with Fort Union in 1866 and 1867 to supply it with livestock and forage. (I must thank Leo Oliva for finally shedding light on the corral's origins in his colossal publication, *Fort Union and the Frontier Army in the Southwest,* 1994.)[5]

Across the interstate from the stage station is sleepy Watrous. Originally, the village was named La Junta because here two waterways—the Mora and Sapello rivers—merged. The name was doubly significant, for the two branches of the Trail also joined here. But, in 1879 when the Atchison, Topeka, and Santa Fe railroad came to town it was renamed because there already was one La Junta on the line, that one being in Colorado. So, the railroad selected the name Watrous to honor the town's founder. Good choice, in my judgment. Sam Watrous built a twenty room house and store at the north end of town in 1849, and conducted a lucrative trade with Trail travelers. The town was the rendezvous point where eastbound wagon trains formed—the counterpart of Council Grove in eastern Kansas where westbound caravans organized. Sam's abode still stands, although greatly remodeled as the handsome headquarters of the Doolittle Ranch. Often I have pulled into the entrance to the driveway, looked long and hard at the contemporary ranch style house, trying to determine just where the original is hiding behind that whitewashed exterior. Supposedly, the store is contained within the front right end as one faces the dwelling. Continuing past the ranch, the road plunges into a tunnel of giant Black Willow trees that line both sides. Sam brought these trees over the Trail when they were but tiny seedlings.

Still a few more years later, I had several opportunities to explore the house, thanks to the courteous owner, Barbara Doolittle. I also learned that most of the house's exterior structure is original, although it has been remodeled both inside and out. The style is traditional southwest—a modified square shape with a placita, or courtyard, at the center. All of the rooms open to a continuous portal facing the placita. It has also been reported on the best authority that the trees lining the road are New Mexico natives, and did not travel the Trail.

Doubling back about one mile from the ranch, one enters the town proper. Although possibly only one building, that being the once elegant but now crumbling Masonic hall, dates to Trail days, the village itself is an interesting montage of traditional northern New Mexico architecture. On one of my earlier visits here, as I slowly drove around the town, I came upon an opossum leisurely ambling across a dirt street and then into the yard of a small house. Was this a pet or a wild creature spending a day in Watrous?

On this January excursion we simply drove straight through town and back onto the interstate. It was time to "noon," so we drove the few miles northeast to the fine rest stop featuring its territorial style center, passing a long stretch of pristine ruts en route. The last time I passed this way a large herd of antelope was strolling down the Trail. When we reached the rest stop, heavy snow-laden clouds had moved in from the north, and a sharp wind had come up. Not the most ideal picnicking conditions, so we ate quickly and scurried back to the warmth of the car. This experience provided yet another stark contrast between following the Trail in the twentieth century as opposed to the nineteenth. We could find comfort in a toasty Cherokee, whereas Trail travelers had the luxury of a warm fire only after the train had stopped. When on the move, they had to rely totally on warm clothing.

Note: Thirteen miles north of Wagon Mound is the Mora Ranch road leading to Ocate Creek Crossing. The area contains a collection of impressive Trail sites which had escaped my attention on my early Trail treks. When I finally visited it I was so amazed that I returned again and again. The creek sits at the base of Apache Mesa over which the Mountain Route coursed, heading toward Santa Fe. Excellent ruts are visible both on the mesa and on the rangeland below. One of many outstanding End of the Trail field trips centered at the site. We shared the pasture with a herd of yearlings who ran eagerly toward our auto caravan, expecting to be fed.

The ruins of a trading post and pioneer cemetery were situated back from the creek bank. We drove up the narrow ranch road to the mesa top, which commanded a sweeping view westward toward Fort Union.

On another visit, my auto ignition suddenly failed on the mesa during our walk in the ruts. The nearest *possible*, though by no means guaranteed, sign of humanity was five miles in either direction—not good prospects on a Sunday afternoon. My friend, Faith Blakely, suggested that we eat lunch and try later. Her advice was sound, and the engine promptly responded when I tried later.

Returning to our present journey, our next destination was to have been Point of Rocks, forty miles northeast of Springer, ten miles which are a poor grade dirt road. However, by the time we rolled into Springer, the first snowflakes began to fall. Should we continue on or turn back? We elected to decide over a cup of hot coffee at the Brown Bed and Breakfast, well known throughout all of northeastern New Mexico. This being Sunday, the restaurant was crowded. The jovial waitress gave us the Chamber of Commerce description of all the local attractions. The only problem—none were open. Thus, touring Springer was not a viable backup plan to Point of Rocks, particularly in winter. She suggested we come back in summer, but we should be sure to call ahead. By the time we had finished our second cup of coffee and a piece of pie, the snow was getting serious. Sadly, I aimed the Cherokee back to Santa Fe, being forced to save Point of Rocks for another day.

The snow abated by the time we reached Las Vegas, so we toured the Old Town Plaza and a few nearby sites. Being in the area, I had to swing by Kearny Gap and Puertocito Pedregosa, particularly since Joan had not been there before. The snow and muddy road precluded a walk in those deep ruts between these two natural passes, but that did not diminish the dramatic views.

When Santa Fe hove into view an hour later, dusk had descended. It had been a full and exciting day along the Trail, the aborted Point of Rocks stop notwithstanding. My feelings are best expressed by Josiah Gregg as he witnessed, "wagon after wagon...pouring down the last declivity...from [Santa Fe].... To judge from the clamorous rejoicings of the men...the spectacle must have been as new to them as it had been to me.... Even the animals seemed to participate in the humor of their riders...."[6]

As I write this, with great sadness I note that this was Demi's last Trail trip. Two months later she was dead.

Notes

1. Myres, Sandra L. (Ed.). *Cavalry Wife: The Diary of Eveline M. Alexander, 1866–1867.* College Station, Texas: Texas A & M University Press, 1977, p. 111.

2. Drumm, Stella (Ed.). *Down the Santa Fe Trail and Into Mexico: The Diary of Susan Magoffin, 1846–1847.* Lincoln, Nebraska: University of Nebraska Press, 1982, p. 99.

3. Russell, Marion Sloan. *Land of Enchantment: Memoirs of Marion Russell Along the Santa Fe Trail As Dictated to Mrs. Hal Russell.* Albuquerque, New Mexico: University of New Mexico Press, 1981, p. 48.

4. Major John C. McFarran's Report and Journal. In Marc Simmons (Ed.), *On the Santa Fe Trail.* Lawrence, Kansas: University Press of Kansas, 1986

5. Oliva, Leo E., *Fort Union and the Frontier Army in the Southwest.* Santa Fe, New Mexico: Division of History, National Park Service, 1993.

6. Gregg, Josiah. *The Commerce of the Prairies.* Milo Milton Quaife (Ed.). Lincoln, Nebraska: University of Nebraska Press, 1967, pgs. 101-2.

I-25 ruts, Las Vegas, New Mexico.

Kearny Gap stage station ruins, Las Vegas, New Mexico.

Apache Ridge, Cañoncito, New Mexico.

Apache Ridge construction, Cañoncito, New Mexico.

Loma Parda, New Mexico.

Apache Mesa ruts, New Mexico.

Apache Mesa ruts, New Mexico.

Afterword

How should I bring closure to this odyssey? For some time this question has been lurking about in the recesses of my consciousness. Yet, every time I attempt to deal with it I recall some experience that I have failed to record; or, more likely, I have been out on the Trail yet another time discovering yet another site new to me, and thereby creating more memories. Many weekends, for example, I considered going to Pecos National Historic Park to see if the ranger would finally allow me to see those ruts below the mission church ruins.

What more could I learn about the Trail—and myself, in fact—aside from accumulating more historical facts, if another new-found site emerged on the horizon? Is this a continuous "work in progress" these hundred thirty plus years after the last wagon came to a halt? Is the Trail forever with us, a fabric of our very being? No doubt, the Trail has changed me, and definitely for the better. The essence of my being has definitely expanded through the interactions with the many incredible people who have come within my purview. Walking the ruts, standing on a creek bank, strolling through a cemetery, or visually following a line in the dirt into the distance—all this and more often float around in my mind. You see, the Santa Fe Trail is not simply a place in time. It is a mental concept shrouded in material substance existing over a specific period of time.

Historian Marc Simmons said it best, "The Santa Fe Trail lives on!"

Bibliography

Books:

Barbour, Barton H. (Ed.). *Reluctant Frontiersman: James Ross Larkin on the Santa Fe Trail 1856–1857*. Albuquerque, New Mexico: University of New Mexico Press, 1990.

Barry, Louise. *The Beginning of the West: Annals of the Kansas Gateway to the American West 1540–1854*. Topeka, Kansas: Kansas State Historical Society, 1972.

Cook, Mary J. Straw. *Loretto: The Sisters and Their Chapel*. Santa Fe, New Mexico: Museum of New Mexico Press, 2002.

Davis, W.W.H. *El Gringo: New Mexico and Her People*. Lincoln, Nebraska: University of Nebraska Press, 1982.

Drumm, Stella (Ed.). *Down the Santa Fe Trail and Into Mexico: The Diary of Susan Magoffin, 1846–1847*. Lincoln, Nebraska: University of Nebraska Press, 1982.

Elder, Jane L., and David J. Weber (Eds.). *Trading in Santa Fe*. Dallas, Texas: Southern Methodist University Press, 1996.

Franzwa, Gregory. *The Santa Fe Trail Revisited*. St. Louis, Missouri: The Patrice Press, 1989.

Fraser, J. T. *Time, the Familiar Stranger*. Redmond, Washington: Tempus Books, 1987.

Garrard, Lewis. *Wah-to-yah on the Taos Trail*. Norman, Oklahoma: University of Oklahoma Press, 1955.

Gregg, Josiah. *The Commerce of the Prairies*. Milo Milton Quaife (Ed.). Lincoln, Nebraska: University of Nebraska Press, 1967.

Gregg, Kate L. *The Road to Santa Fe: The Journal and Diaries of* George *Champlin Sibley*. Albuquerque, New Mexico: University of New Mexico Press, 1952

Hyslop, Stephen G. *Bound for Santa Fe: The Road to New Mexico and the American Conquest, 1806–1848*. Norman, Oklahoma: University of Oklahoma Press, 2002.

Lane, Lydia Spencer. *I Married a Soldier*. Albuquerque, New Mexico: University of New Mexico Press, 1987.

Lavender, David. *Bent's Fort*. Lincoln, Nebraska: University of Nebraska Press, 1954.

Majors, Alexander. *Seventy Years on the Frontier*. Lincoln, Nebraska: University of Nebraska Press, 1989.

Myres, Sandra L. (Ed.). *Cavalry Wife. The Diary of Eveline M. Alexander, 1866–1867*. College Station, Texas: Texas A & M University Press, 1977.

Napton, W.B. *Over the Santa Fe Trail in 1857*. Arrow Rock, Missouri: Friends of Arrow Rock, 1991.

Oliva, Leo E. *Fort Union and the Frontier Army in the Southwest*. Santa Fe, New Mexico: Division of History, National Park Service, 1993.

Russell, Marion Sloan. *Land of Enchantment: Memoirs of Marion Russell Along the Santa Fe Trail as Dictated to Mrs. Hal Russell*. Albuquerque, New Mexico: University of New Mexico Press , 1981.

Simmons, Marc. *Following the Santa Fe Trail.* Santa Fe, New Mexico: Ancient City Press, 1986.

Simmons, Marc, and Joan Myers. *Along the Santa Fe Trail.* Albuquerque, New Mexico: University of New Mexico Press, 1986.

Strate, David K. (Ed.). *West by Southwest: Letters of Joseph Pratt Allyn, Traveller Along the Santa Fe Trail, 1863.* Dodge City, Kansas: Heritage Center, 1984.

Sunder, John (Ed.). *Matt Field on the Santa Fe Trail.* Norman, Oklahoma: University of Oklahoma Press, 1960.

Van Tramp, John C. *Prairie and Rocky Mountain Adventures, 1858.* In William Least Heat-Moon, *PrairyErth.* Boston, Massachusetts: Houghton Mifflin, 1991.

Vestal, Stanley. *The Old Santa Fe Trail.* Boston, Massachusetts: Houghton Mifflin, 1939.

Pamphlets and Booklets:

Brigham, Lalla Maloy. *The Story of Council Grove on the Santa Fe Trail.* Council Grove: Morris County Historical Society, 1921.

Colle, Britt and Linda. Trail Booklet, Santa Fe Trail Association Symposium, 2005.

Fort Larned. National Park Service, Interpretive brochure, 1987.

"Like a Ribbon Across the Prairie," Cimarron, Kiowa and Comanche National Grasslands brochure.

Articles in Edited Works:

David Kellogg's Diary, 1858. In Marc Simmons (Ed.) *On the Santa Fe Trail.* Lawrence, Kansas: University Press of Kansas, 1986.

Major John C. McFarran's Report and Journal. In Marc Simmons (Ed.), *On the Santa Fe Trail.* Lawrence, Kansas: University Press of Kansas, 1986.

Schulz, Ray S. Murder, Massacre, and Misfortune Near Walnut Creek Crossing. In Leo E. Oliva (Ed.) *Confrontation on the Santa Fe Trail,* Larned, Kansas: Santa Fe Trail Association, 1996.

Michael Speck, 1852, Trail Letter by. In Marc Simmons (Ed.) *On the Santa Fe Trail.* Lawrence, Kansas: University Press of Kansas. 1986.

Journals:

Chadwick, Douglas. The American Prairie. *National Geographic,* 1993, Vol. 184, Issue 4, p. 99.

Davis, H. Denny. Franklin: Cradle of the Trade. *Wagon Tracks,* 1993, Vol. 7, Issue 3, pp. 11-17.

Fisher, Virginia. Tabo Creek. *Wagon Tracks,* 1991, Vol. 5, Issue 3, pp. 8-9.

Maier, M.A. Pecan Time. *New Mexico,* November, 1993.

Mooney, Sylvia D. Cave Spring: Historic Landmark on the Santa Fe Trail. *Wagon Tracks,* 1988, Vol. 3, Issue 1, p. 7.

Moore, John W. Trail Trip, 1867. In *Dawson Scrapbooks,* "Trails and Forts." *Wagon Tracks,* 1990, Vol. 4, Issue 2, p. 17.

Olsen, Michael and Harry C. Myers, The Diary of Pedro Ignacio Gallego Wherein 400 Soldiers Following Comanches met William Becknell on his First Trip to Santa Fe. *Wagon Tracks*, 1992, Vol. 7, Issue 1, pp. 15-20.

Texan-Santa Fe Expedition. *Wagon Tracks*, 1989, Vol. 4, Issue 1, p. 15.

www.ingramcontent.com/pod-product-compliance
Lightning Source LLC
Chambersburg PA
CBHW022008080426
42733CB00007B/521